Contents

Literacy Centers—Take It to Your Seat • EMC 2724 • ©2004 by Evan-Moor Corp.

About Literacy Centers
Grades 4–5

What's Great About This Book

Centers are a wonderful, fun way for students to practice important skills. The 16 centers in this book are self-contained and portable. Students may work at a desk, table, or even on the floor. Once you've made the centers, they're ready to use any time.

What's in This Book

Teacher direction page includes a description of the student task

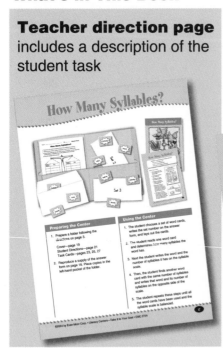

Full-color materials needed for the center

Reproducible answer forms

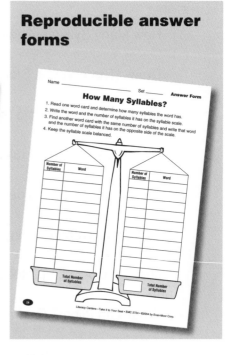

How to Use the Centers

The centers are intended for skill practice, not to introduce skills. It is important to model the use of each center before students do the task independently.

Questions to Consider:

- Will students select a center, or will you assign the centers?
- Will there be a specific block of time for centers, or will the centers be used throughout the day?
- Where will you place the centers for easy access by students?
- What procedure will students use when they need help with the center tasks?
- Where will students store completed work?
- How will you track the tasks and centers completed by each student?

Literacy Centers—Take It to Your Seat • EMC 2724 • ©2004 by Evan-Moor Corp.

Making a File Folder Center

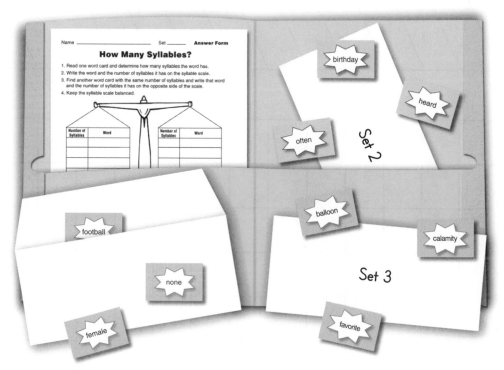

Materials

- folder with pockets
- envelopes or plastic self-locking bags
- marking pens and pencils
- scissors
- two-sided tape

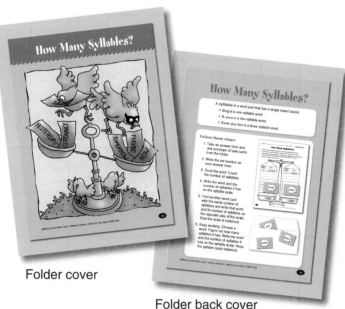

Folder cover

Folder back cover
Student Direction page

Steps to Follow

1. Laminate the cover. Tape it to the front of the folder.

2. Laminate the student direction page. Tape it to the back of the folder.

3. Place answer forms, writing paper, and any other supplies in the left-hand pocket.

4. Laminate the task cards. Place each set of cards in a labeled envelope or plastic self-locking bag. Place the envelopes and sorting mat (if required for the center) in the right-hand pocket.

Folder centers are easily stored in a box or file crate. Students take a folder to their desks to complete the task.

Center Checklist

Student Names

Centers

What Does It Mean?													
How Many Syllables?													
Draw...Then Write a Story													
Name the Relationship													
Where Can I Find It?													
Word Pictures													
Groups of Three													
Just the Opposite													
What's an Idiom?													
Two into One													
Fix It Up!													
Pattern a Poem													
Get to the Root of It													
Here's How to Do It!													
Making Sense of Sentences													
One Word—Two Meanings													

What Does It Mean?

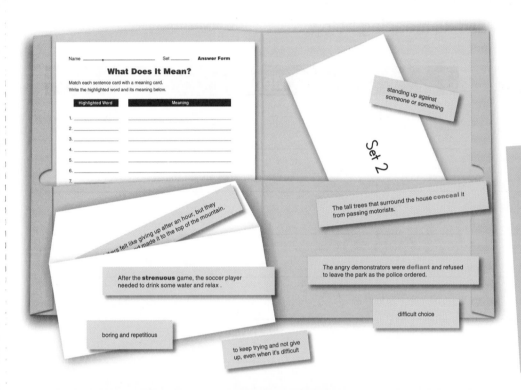

Preparing the Center

1. Prepare a folder following the directions on page 3.

   Cover—page 7
   Student Directions—page 9
   Task Cards—pages 11–15

2. Reproduce a supply of the answer form on page 6. Place copies in the left-hand pocket of the folder.

3. Match the sentence cards and meaning cards by color to make a set. Place each set in an envelope and label it with the set number. Place the envelopes in the right-hand pocket of the folder.

Using the Center

1. The student selects a set of cards and writes the set number on the answer form.

2. Next, the student sorts and lays out the sentence cards and the meaning cards. The student reads a sentence and matches it to the meaning card that defines the highlighted word in the sentence.

3. Finally, the student copies the highlighted word and its meaning onto the answer form.

What Does It Mean?

Match each sentence card with a meaning card.

Write the highlighted word and its meaning below.

Highlighted Word	Meaning
1. _____	_____
2. _____	_____
3. _____	_____
4. _____	_____
5. _____	_____
6. _____	_____
7. _____	_____
8. _____	_____

Bonus: Using one of the highlighted words, write and illustrate a new sentence below.

What Does It Mean?

What Does It Mean?

Use the **context**, the words before and after the highlighted word, to determine its meaning.

Follow these steps:

1. Take an answer form and one envelope of task cards from the folder.

2. Write the set number on your answer form.

3. Sort the task cards into two piles: sentence cards and meaning cards. Lay them out.

4. Read a sentence card. Use the context to figure out the meaning of the highlighted word.

5. Find the meaning card that matches the meaning of the highlighted word.

6. Repeat for each sentence card.

7. Write each highlighted word and its meaning on the answer form.

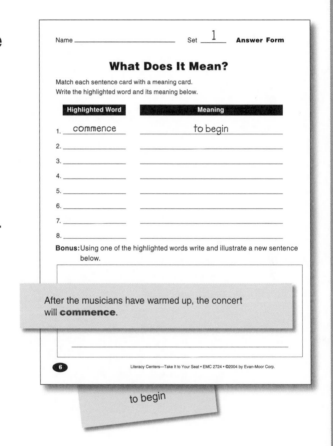

The bikers felt like giving up after an hour, but they **persevered** and made it to the top of the mountain.

Picking up every tiny piece of confetti off the carpet is a **tedious** job.

The picnic by the lake turned **dismal** when the storm clouds filled the sky.

After the **strenuous** game, the soccer player needed to drink some water and relax.

One **consequence** of not turning in assignments might be getting a poor grade.

After the musicians have warmed up, the concert will **commence**.

Microwave dinners are very **convenient** because you can quickly and easily prepare a meal in minutes.

Timothy did such a **thorough** job cleaning the easel that there wasn't a speck of paint left.

What Does It Mean?
Set 1

©2004 by Evan-Moor Corp. • EMC 2724

What Does It Mean?
Set 1

©2004 by Evan-Moor Corp. • EMC 2724

What Does It Mean?
Set 1

©2004 by Evan-Moor Corp. • EMC 2724

What Does It Mean?
Set 1

©2004 by Evan-Moor Corp. • EMC 2724

What Does It Mean?
Set 1

©2004 by Evan-Moor Corp. • EMC 2724

What Does It Mean?
Set 1

©2004 by Evan-Moor Corp. • EMC 2724

What Does It Mean?
Set 1

©2004 by Evan-Moor Corp. • EMC 2724

What Does It Mean?
Set 1

©2004 by Evan-Moor Corp. • EMC 2724

Peter's **dilemma** was whether to wear his heavy jacket or his windbreaker to the game.

Most communities have a program to feed and clothe people who are **destitute**.

The still, smelly water remained **stagnant** until it rained.

The angry demonstrators were **defiant** and refused to leave the park as the police ordered.

The **ingenious** cook made a delicious stew from the leftovers in the refrigerator.

The City Council spent many months planning new construction and repairs to **renovate** the old playground.

The tall trees that surround the house **conceal** it from passing motorists.

When the man could no longer **tolerate** the child kicking his seat, he turned around and asked him to stop.

What Does It Mean?

Set 2

©2004 by Evan-Moor Corp. • EMC 2724

What Does It Mean?

Set 2

©2004 by Evan-Moor Corp. • EMC 2724

What Does It Mean?

Set 2

©2004 by Evan-Moor Corp. • EMC 2724

What Does It Mean?

Set 2

©2004 by Evan-Moor Corp. • EMC 2724

What Does It Mean?

Set 2

©2004 by Evan-Moor Corp. • EMC 2724

What Does It Mean?

Set 2

©2004 by Evan-Moor Corp. • EMC 2724

What Does It Mean?

Set 2

©2004 by Evan-Moor Corp. • EMC 2724

What Does It Mean?

Set 2

©2004 by Evan-Moor Corp. • EMC 2724

to keep trying and not give up, even when it's difficult	difficult choice
boring and repetitious	without food, shelter, or money
dark and gloomy	not active, changing, or developing
requiring a lot of strength and energy	standing up against someone or something
what happens as a result of another action	clever or skillful
to begin	to make like new
useful, easy, and no trouble	to hide, disguise, or keep secret
careful and complete	to be able to put up with something

What Does It Mean?

Set 2

©2004 by Evan-Moor Corp. • EMC 2724

What Does It Mean?

Set 2

©2004 by Evan-Moor Corp. • EMC 2724

What Does It Mean?

Set 2

©2004 by Evan-Moor Corp. • EMC 2724

What Does It Mean?

Set 2

©2004 by Evan-Moor Corp. • EMC 2724

What Does It Mean?

Set 2

©2004 by Evan-Moor Corp. • EMC 2724

What Does It Mean?

Set 2

©2004 by Evan-Moor Corp. • EMC 2724

What Does It Mean?

Set 2

©2004 by Evan-Moor Corp. • EMC 2724

What Does It Mean?

Set 2

©2004 by Evan-Moor Corp. • EMC 2724

What Does It Mean?

Set 1

©2004 by Evan-Moor Corp. • EMC 2724

What Does It Mean?

Set 1

©2004 by Evan-Moor Corp. • EMC 2724

What Does It Mean?

Set 1

©2004 by Evan-Moor Corp. • EMC 2724

What Does It Mean?

Set 1

©2004 by Evan-Moor Corp. • EMC 2724

What Does It Mean?

Set 1

©2004 by Evan-Moor Corp. • EMC 2724

What Does It Mean?

Set 1

©2004 by Evan-Moor Corp. • EMC 2724

What Does It Mean?

Set 1

©2004 by Evan-Moor Corp. • EMC 2724

What Does It Mean?

Set 1

©2004 by Evan-Moor Corp. • EMC 2724

How Many Syllables?

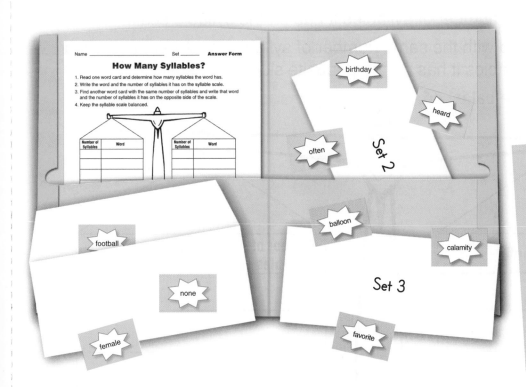

Preparing the Center

1. Prepare a folder following the directions on page 3.

   Cover—page 19
   Student Directions—page 21
   Task Cards—pages 23–27

2. Reproduce a supply of the answer form on page 18. Place copies in the left-hand pocket of the folder.

Using the Center

1. The student chooses a set of word cards, writes the set number on the answer form, and lays out the cards.

2. The student reads one word card and determines how many syllables the word has.

3. Next, the student writes the word and the number of syllables it has on the syllable scale.

4. Then the student finds another word card with the same number of syllables and writes that word and its number of syllables on the opposite side of the scale.

5. The student repeats these steps until all the word cards have been used and the syllable scale is balanced.

Name _____   Set _____

How Many Syllables?

1. Read one word card and determine how many syllables the word has.

2. Write the word and the number of syllables it has on the syllable scale.

3. Find another word card with the same number of syllables and write that word and the number of syllables it has on the opposite side of the scale.

4. Keep the syllable scale balanced.

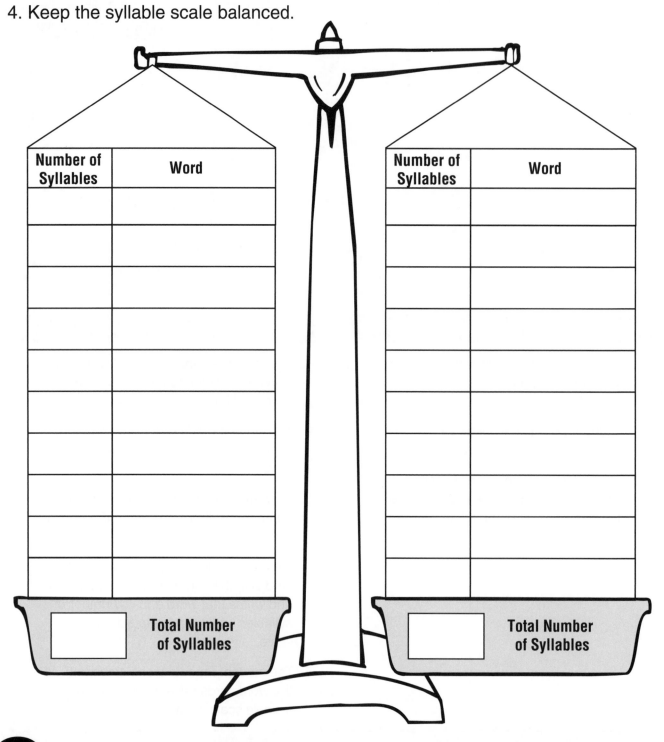

Number of Syllables	Word

Number of Syllables	Word

Total Number of Syllables

Total Number of Syllables

How Many Syllables?

How Many Syllables?

A **syllable** is a word part that has a single vowel sound.

- **Dog** is a one-syllable word.
- **O·pen** is a two-syllable word.
- **Com·pu·ter** is a three-syllable word.

Follow these steps:

1. Take an answer form and one envelope of task cards from the folder.

2. Write the set number on your answer form.

3. Read the word. Count the number of syllables.

4. Write the word and the number of syllables it has on the syllable scale.

5. Find another word card with the same number of syllables and write that word and its number of syllables on the opposite side of the scale. Now the scale is balanced.

6. Keep working. Choose a word. Figure out how many syllables it has. Write the word and the number of syllables it has on the syllable scale. Keep the syllable scale balanced.

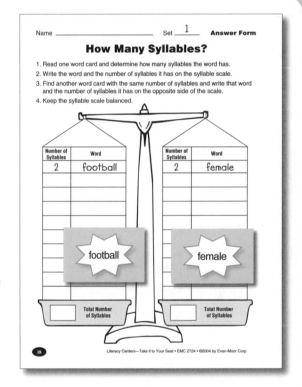

football

about

already

chocolate

said

category

testimony

because

practice

curiosity

university

terrible

excellent

responsibility

availability

female

merchant

How Many Syllables?

Set 1

EMC 2724
©2004 by Evan-Moor Corp.

How Many Syllables?

Set 1

EMC 2724
©2004 by Evan-Moor Corp.

How Many Syllables?

Set 1

EMC 2724
©2004 by Evan-Moor Corp.

How Many Syllables?

Set 1

EMC 2724
©2004 by Evan-Moor Corp.

How Many Syllables?

Set 1

EMC 2724
©2004 by Evan-Moor Corp.

How Many Syllables?

Set 1

EMC 2724
©2004 by Evan-Moor Corp.

How Many Syllables?

Set 1

EMC 2724
©2004 by Evan-Moor Corp.

How Many Syllables?

Set 1

EMC 2724
©2004 by Evan-Moor Corp.

How Many Syllables?

Set 1

EMC 2724
©2004 by Evan-Moor Corp.

How Many Syllables?

Set 1

EMC 2724
©2004 by Evan-Moor Corp.

How Many Syllables?

Set 1

EMC 2724
©2004 by Evan-Moor Corp.

How Many Syllables?

Set 1

EMC 2724
©2004 by Evan-Moor Corp.

How Many Syllables?

Set 1

EMC 2724
©2004 by Evan-Moor Corp.

How Many Syllables?

Set 1

EMC 2724
©2004 by Evan-Moor Corp.

How Many Syllables?

Set 1

EMC 2724
©2004 by Evan-Moor Corp.

How Many Syllables?

Set 1

EMC 2724
©2004 by Evan-Moor Corp.

How Many Syllables?

Set 1

EMC 2724
©2004 by Evan-Moor Corp.

How Many Syllables?

Set 1

EMC 2724
©2004 by Evan-Moor Corp.

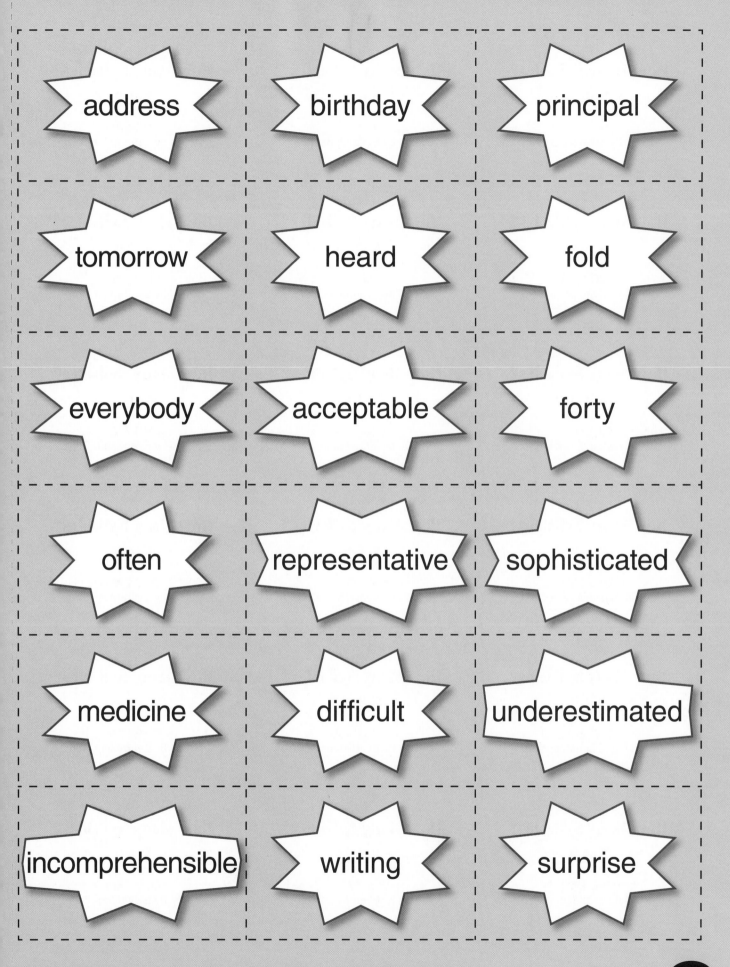

address

birthday

principal

tomorrow

heard

fold

everybody

acceptable

forty

often

representative

sophisticated

medicine

difficult

underestimated

incomprehensible

writing

surprise

How Many Syllables?
Set 2
EMC 2724
©2004 by Evan-Moor Corp.

How Many Syllables?
Set 2
EMC 2724
©2004 by Evan-Moor Corp.

How Many Syllables?
Set 2
EMC 2724
©2004 by Evan-Moor Corp.

How Many Syllables?
Set 2
EMC 2724
©2004 by Evan-Moor Corp.

How Many Syllables?
Set 2
EMC 2724
©2004 by Evan-Moor Corp.

How Many Syllables?
Set 2
EMC 2724
©2004 by Evan-Moor Corp.

How Many Syllables?
Set 2
EMC 2724
©2004 by Evan-Moor Corp.

How Many Syllables?
Set 2
EMC 2724
©2004 by Evan-Moor Corp.

How Many Syllables?
Set 2
EMC 2724
©2004 by Evan-Moor Corp.

How Many Syllables?
Set 2
EMC 2724
©2004 by Evan-Moor Corp.

How Many Syllables?
Set 2
EMC 2724
©2004 by Evan-Moor Corp.

How Many Syllables?
Set 2
EMC 2724
©2004 by Evan-Moor Corp.

How Many Syllables?
Set 2
EMC 2724
©2004 by Evan-Moor Corp.

How Many Syllables?
Set 2
EMC 2724
©2004 by Evan-Moor Corp.

How Many Syllables?
Set 2
EMC 2724
©2004 by Evan-Moor Corp.

How Many Syllables?
Set 2
EMC 2724
©2004 by Evan-Moor Corp.

How Many Syllables?
Set 2
EMC 2724
©2004 by Evan-Moor Corp.

How Many Syllables?
Set 2
EMC 2724
©2004 by Evan-Moor Corp.

pronunciation

balloon

computer

handkerchief

your

bought

calamity

explanation

answered

sometime

favorite

traveling

experimentation

inferiority

people

cafeteria

capitalize

certificate

How Many Syllables? Set 3 EMC 2724 ©2004 by Evan-Moor Corp.	How Many Syllables? Set 3 EMC 2724 ©2004 by Evan-Moor Corp.	How Many Syllables? Set 3 EMC 2724 ©2004 by Evan-Moor Corp.
How Many Syllables? Set 3 EMC 2724 ©2004 by Evan-Moor Corp.	How Many Syllables? Set 3 EMC 2724 ©2004 by Evan-Moor Corp.	How Many Syllables? Set 3 EMC 2724 ©2004 by Evan-Moor Corp.
How Many Syllables? Set 3 EMC 2724 ©2004 by Evan-Moor Corp.	How Many Syllables? Set 3 EMC 2724 ©2004 by Evan-Moor Corp.	How Many Syllables? Set 3 EMC 2724 ©2004 by Evan-Moor Corp.
How Many Syllables? Set 3 EMC 2724 ©2004 by Evan-Moor Corp.	How Many Syllables? Set 3 EMC 2724 ©2004 by Evan-Moor Corp.	How Many Syllables? Set 3 EMC 2724 ©2004 by Evan-Moor Corp.
How Many Syllables? Set 3 EMC 2724 ©2004 by Evan-Moor Corp.	How Many Syllables? Set 3 EMC 2724 ©2004 by Evan-Moor Corp.	How Many Syllables? Set 3 EMC 2724 ©2004 by Evan-Moor Corp.
How Many Syllables? Set 3 EMC 2724 ©2004 by Evan-Moor Corp.	How Many Syllables? Set 3 EMC 2724 ©2004 by Evan-Moor Corp.	How Many Syllables? Set 3 EMC 2724 ©2004 by Evan-Moor Corp.

Draw...Then Write a Story

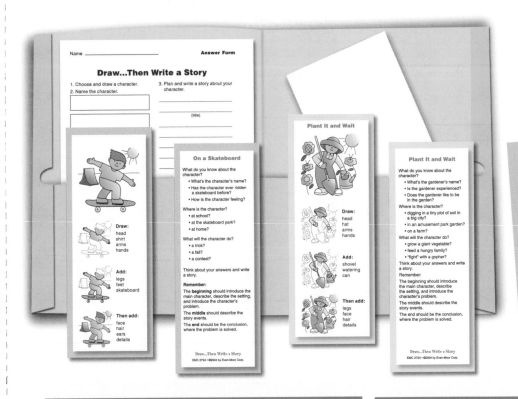

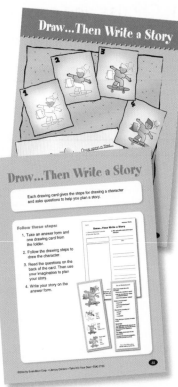

Preparing the Center

1. Prepare a folder following the directions on page 3.

   Cover—page 31
   Student Directions—page 33
   Task Cards—pages 35–39

2. Reproduce a supply of the answer form on page 30. Place copies in the left-hand pocket of the folder along with writing paper.

Using the Center

1. The student takes an answer form and selects a drawing card.

2. Next, the student follows the steps on the card to draw a character.

3. Then the student uses his or her imagination to answer the questions on the card.

4. Finally, the student plans and writes a story.

Name _____

Draw...Then Write a Story

1. Choose and draw a character.

2. Name the character.

3. Plan and write a story about your character.

_____

_____
(title)

_____

_____

_____

_____

_____

_____

_____

_____

_____

_____

_____

_____

Bonus: On the back of this form, draw the character again. Show something that happened in your story.

Draw...Then Write a Story

Once upon a time...

Draw...Then Write a Story

Each drawing card gives the steps for drawing a character and asks questions to help you plan a story.

Follow these steps:

1. Take an answer form and one drawing card from the folder.

2. Follow the drawing steps to draw the character.

3. Read the questions on the back of the card. Then use your imagination to plan your story.

4. Write your story on the answer form.

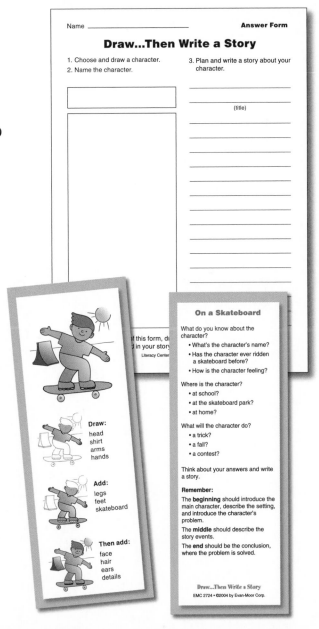

On a Skateboard

Draw:

head
shirt
arms
hands

Add:

legs
feet
skateboard

Then add:

face
hair
ears
details

In Shining Armor

Draw:

helmet
shield

Add:

face
vest armor
arm
spear

Then add:

legs
feet
details

In Shining Armor

What do you know about the character?

- What's the knight's name?
- Does the knight like the armor?
- Is the knight brave or timid?

Where is the character?

- deep in the forest?
- at the mouth of the dragon's cave?
- standing before the king?

What will the character do?

- rescue a damsel in distress?
- complete a task assigned by the king?
- try something never done before?

Think about your answers and write a story.

Remember:

The **beginning** should introduce the main character, describe the setting, and introduce the character's problem.

The **middle** should describe the story events.

The **end** should be the conclusion, where the problem is solved.

Draw...Then Write a Story

EMC 2724 • ©2004 by Evan-Moor Corp.

On a Skateboard

What do you know about the character?

- What's the character's name?
- Has the character ever ridden a skateboard before?
- How is the character feeling?

Where is the character?

- at school?
- at the skateboard park?
- at home?

What will the character do?

- a trick?
- a fall?
- a contest?

Think about your answers and write a story.

Remember:

The **beginning** should introduce the main character, describe the setting, and introduce the character's problem.

The **middle** should describe the story events.

The **end** should be the conclusion, where the problem is solved.

Draw...Then Write a Story

EMC 2724 • ©2004 by Evan-Moor Corp.

Without Gravity

Draw:

helmet
arms

Add:

legs
feet
hands

Then add:

face
air hose
details

What a Catch!

Draw:

head
arms
hands

Add:

jacket
legs
feet

Then add:

face
hat
fishing rod
details

What a Catch!

What do you know about the character?

- What's the character's name?
- Is the character good at fishing?
- Does the character like to fish?

Where is the character?

- sitting in a rowboat?
- standing by a creek?
- on a fishing boat in the ocean?

What will the character do?

- hook a huge fish?
- reel in a piece of seaweed?
- get the hook caught in a tree?

Think about your answers and write a story.

Remember:

The **beginning** should introduce the main character, describe the setting, and introduce the character's problem.

The **middle** should describe the story events.

The **end** should be the conclusion, where the problem is solved.

Draw...Then Write a Story

EMC 2724 • ©2004 by Evan-Moor Corp.

Without Gravity

What do you know about the character?

- What's the space traveler's name?
- Why is the traveler in space?
- Is the traveler feeling safe?

Where is the character?

- floating away from the spaceship?
- stepping for the first time onto a new planet?
- practicing in the simulator?

What will the character do?

- discover a new form of life?
- communicate with aliens?
- conduct a scientific experiment?

Think about your answers and write a story.

Remember:

The **beginning** should introduce the main character, describe the setting, and introduce the character's problem.

The **middle** should describe the story events.

The **end** should be the conclusion, where the problem is solved.

Draw...Then Write a Story

EMC 2724 • ©2004 by Evan-Moor Corp.

Plant It and Wait

Draw:

head
hat
arms
hands

Add:

shovel
watering
can

Then add:

face
hair
legs
feet
details

Climbing High

Draw:

head
arms
hands
rope
belt

Add:

legs
feet

Then add:

helmet
face
hair
rock face
details

Climbing High

What do you know about the character?

- What's the explorer's name?
- What dangers does the explorer face?
- Is the explorer afraid?

Where is the character?

- in a wild tropical jungle?
- in the frozen desert of the Arctic?
- in a huge unexplored cave?

What will the character do?

- discover a treasure?
- get lost?
- map the unexplored land?

Think about your answers and write a story.

Remember:

The **beginning** should introduce the main character, describe the setting, and introduce the character's problem.

The **middle** should describe the story events.

The **end** should be the conclusion, where the problem is solved.

Draw...Then Write a Story

EMC 2724 • ©2004 by Evan-Moor Corp.

Plant It and Wait

What do you know about the character?

- What's the gardener's name?
- Is the gardener experienced?
- Does the gardener like to be in the garden?

Where is the character?

- digging in a tiny plot of soil in a big city?
- in an amusement park garden?
- on a farm?

What will the character do?

- grow a giant vegetable?
- feed a hungry family?
- "fight" with a gopher?

Think about your answers and write a story.

Remember:

The **beginning** should introduce the main character, describe the setting, and introduce the character's problem.

The **middle** should describe the story events.

The **end** should be the conclusion, where the problem is solved.

Draw...Then Write a Story

EMC 2724 • ©2004 by Evan-Moor Corp.

Name the Relationship

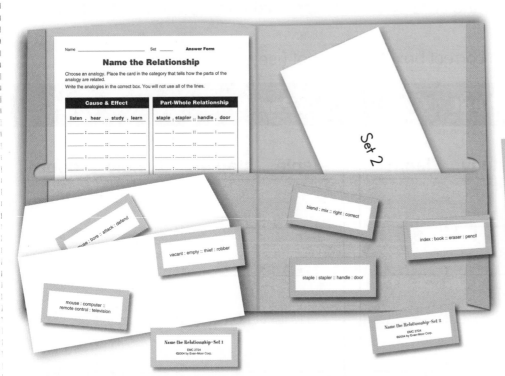

Preparing the Center

1. Prepare a folder following the directions on page 3.

   Cover—page 43
   Student Directions—page 45
   Task Cards—pages 47 and 49

2. Reproduce a supply of the answer form on page 42. Place copies in the left-hand pocket of the folder.

Using the Center

1. The student selects a set of cards and writes the set number on the answer form.

2. Next, the student sorts the analogies by relationships, placing each card in the correct category on the answer form.

3. The student then writes each of the analogies in the proper box on the answer form.

Name _____ Set _____ **Answer Form**

Name the Relationship

Choose an analogy. Place the card in the category that tells how the parts of the analogy are related.

Write the analogies in the correct box. You will not use all of the lines.

Cause & Effect

listen : hear :: study : learn

_____ : _____ :: _____ : _____

_____ : _____ :: _____ : _____

_____ : _____ :: _____ : _____

_____ : _____ :: _____ : _____

Part-Whole Relationship

staple : stapler :: handle : door

_____ : _____ :: _____ : _____

_____ : _____ :: _____ : _____

_____ : _____ :: _____ : _____

_____ : _____ :: _____ : _____

Antonyms

seldom : often :: few : many

_____ : _____ :: _____ : _____

_____ : _____ :: _____ : _____

_____ : _____ :: _____ : _____

_____ : _____ :: _____ : _____

Synonyms

story : tale :: wealth : riches

_____ : _____ :: _____ : _____

_____ : _____ :: _____ : _____

_____ : _____ :: _____ : _____

_____ : _____ :: _____ : _____

Bonus: Write one new analogy for each category.

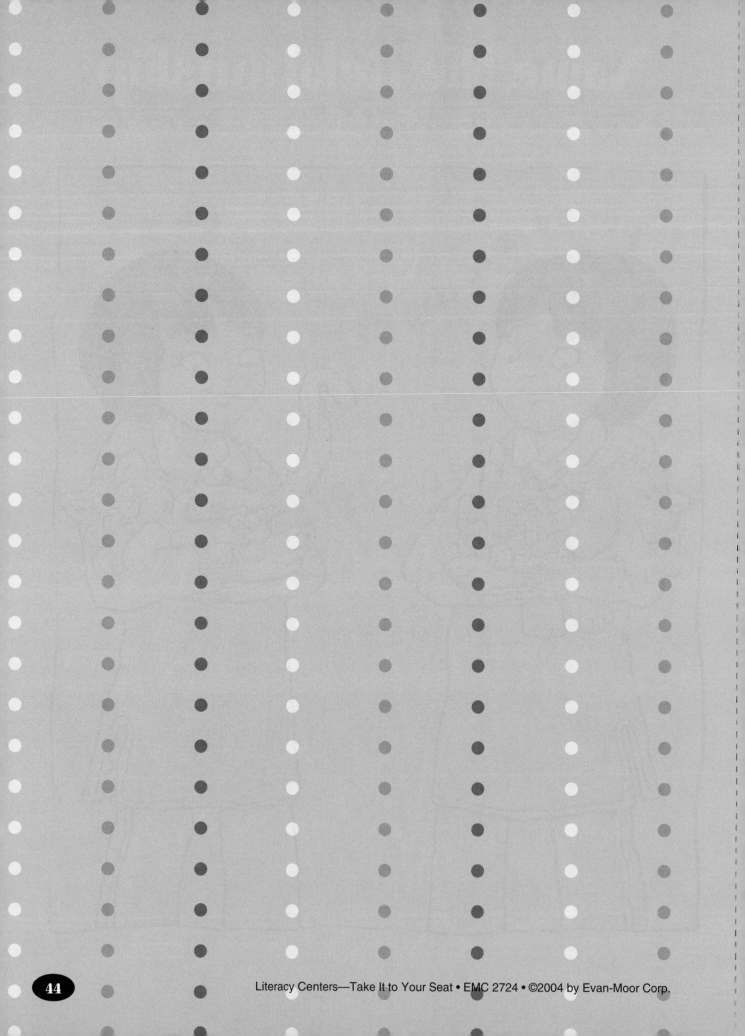

Name the Relationship

An **analogy** is one kind of comparison. It compares one set of objects or ideas with another set of objects or ideas. The ideas must be related to each other in the same way.

Calf is to cow as fawn is to doe.

There is a shorter way to write analogies.

: means is to   :: means as

Calf : cow :: fawn : doe

Follow these steps:

1. Take the answer form and one envelope of task cards from the folder.

2. Write the set number on your answer form.

3. Read one card. Figure out how the sets of objects are related.

4. Place the card in the category that names the relationship.

5. Keep working. Repeat for each card.

6. Write the analogies in the correct box on the answer form. You will not use all of the lines.

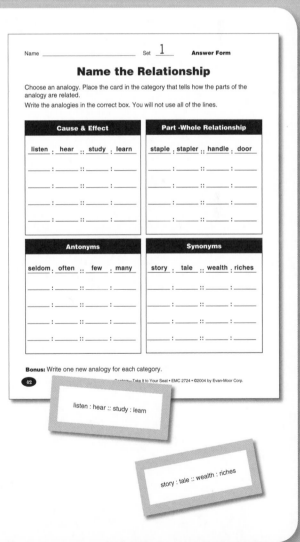

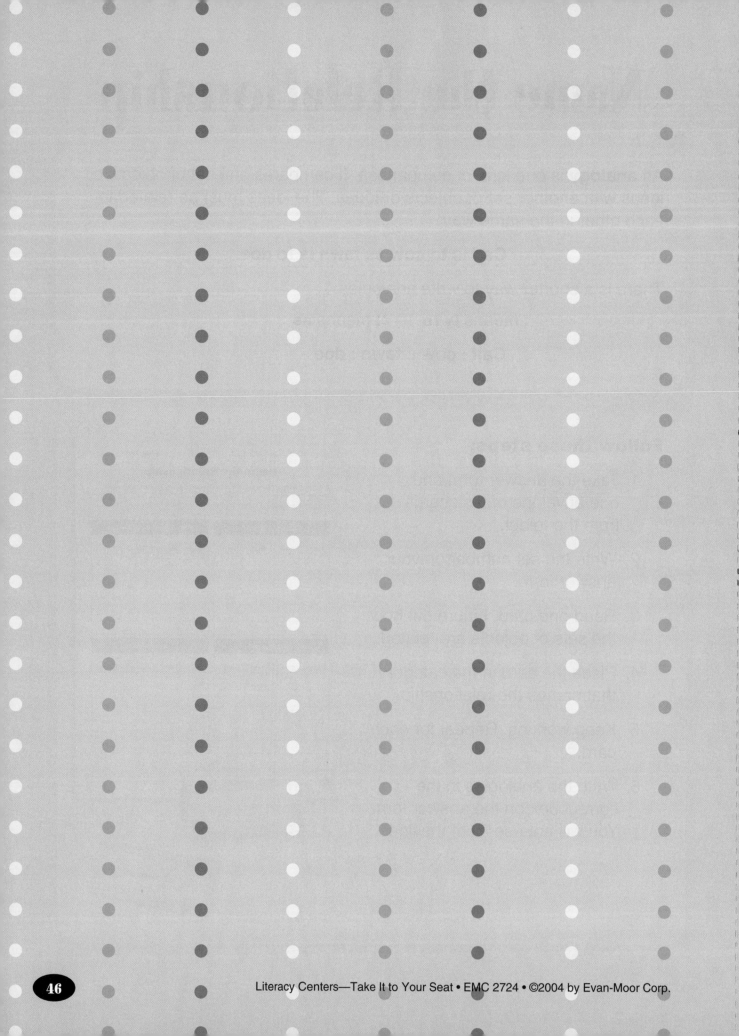

amuse : bore :: attack : defend

awake : asleep :: after : before

misbehavior : punishment ::
oversleeping : tardy

vacant : empty :: thief : robber

lens : camera :: wing : plane

mouse : computer ::
remote control : television

story : tale :: wealth : riches

heat : sweating :: cold : shivering

nail : finger :: eyelash : eye

gift : present :: active : lively

plot : scheme ::
pleasure : enjoyment

listen : hear :: study : learn

Name the Relationship–Set 1

EMC 2724
©2004 by Evan-Moor Corp.

Name the Relationship–Set 1

EMC 2724
©2004 by Evan-Moor Corp.

Name the Relationship–Set 1

EMC 2724
©2004 by Evan-Moor Corp.

Name the Relationship–Set 1

EMC 2724
©2004 by Evan-Moor Corp.

Name the Relationship–Set 1

EMC 2724
©2004 by Evan-Moor Corp.

Name the Relationship–Set 1

EMC 2724
©2004 by Evan-Moor Corp.

Name the Relationship–Set 1

EMC 2724
©2004 by Evan-Moor Corp.

Name the Relationship–Set 1

EMC 2724
©2004 by Evan-Moor Corp.

Name the Relationship–Set 1

EMC 2724
©2004 by Evan-Moor Corp.

Name the Relationship–Set 1

EMC 2724
©2004 by Evan-Moor Corp.

Name the Relationship–Set 1

EMC 2724
©2004 by Evan-Moor Corp.

Name the Relationship–Set 1

EMC 2724
©2004 by Evan-Moor Corp.

answer : question :: alone : together

seldom : often :: few : many

blend : mix :: right : correct

hot : boiling :: cold : freezing

push : fall :: practice : improve

run : tired :: sleep : rested

index : book :: eraser : pencil

lens : camera :: reel : fishing pole

earthquake : damage :: infection : illness

part : portion :: weak : feeble

staple : stapler :: handle : door

fiction : fact :: long : short

Name the Relationship–Set 2

EMC 2724
©2004 by Evan-Moor Corp.

Name the Relationship–Set 2

EMC 2724
©2004 by Evan-Moor Corp.

Name the Relationship–Set 2

EMC 2724
©2004 by Evan-Moor Corp.

Name the Relationship–Set 2

EMC 2724
©2004 by Evan-Moor Corp.

Name the Relationship–Set 2

EMC 2724
©2004 by Evan-Moor Corp.

Name the Relationship–Set 2

EMC 2724
©2004 by Evan-Moor Corp.

Name the Relationship–Set 2

EMC 2724
©2004 by Evan-Moor Corp.

Name the Relationship–Set 2

EMC 2724
©2004 by Evan-Moor Corp.

Name the Relationship–Set 2

EMC 2724
©2004 by Evan-Moor Corp.

Name the Relationship–Set 2

EMC 2724
©2004 by Evan-Moor Corp.

Name the Relationship–Set 2

EMC 2724
©2004 by Evan-Moor Corp.

Where Can I Find It?

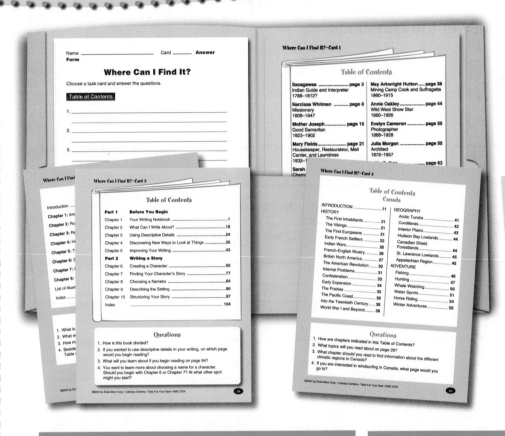
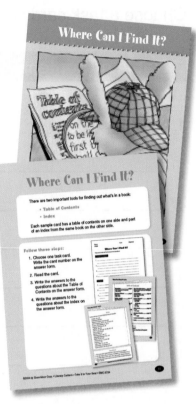

Preparing the Center

1. Prepare a folder following the directions on page 3.

   Cover—page 53
   Student Directions—page 55
   Task Cards—pages 57–63

2. Reproduce a supply of the answer form on page 52. Place copies in the left-hand pocket of the folder.

Using the Center

1. The student selects a task card and writes the card number on the answer form.

2. The student reads the card and answers the questions.

Where Can I Find It?

Choose a task card and answer the questions.

Table of Contents

1. _____
   _____
2. _____
   _____
3. _____
   _____
4. _____

Index

1. _____
   _____
2. _____
   _____
3. _____
   _____
4. _____

Bonus: On the back of this form, explain the difference between an index and a table of contents.

Where Can I Find It?

There are two important tools for finding out what's in a book:

- **Table of Contents**

- **Index**

Each sample card has a table of contents on one side and part of an index from the same book on the other side.

Follow these steps:

1. Choose one task card. Write the card number on the answer form.

2. Read the card.

3. Write the answers to the questions about the Table of Contents on the answer form.

4. Write the answers to the questions about the Index on the answer form.

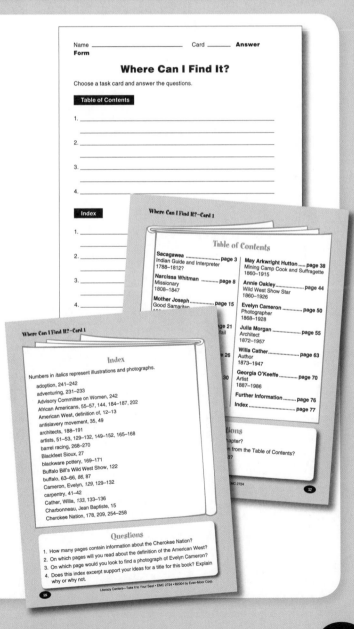

Name _____ Card _____ **Answer Form**

Where Can I Find It?
Choose a task card and answer the questions.

Table of Contents

1. _____
2. _____
3. _____
4. _____

Index

1. _____
2. _____
3. _____
4. _____

Where Can I Find It?—Card 1

Table of Contents

Sacagawea .... page 3
Indian Guide and Interpreter
1788–1812?

Narcissa Whitman .... page 8
Missionary
1808–1847

Mother Joseph .... page 15
Good Samaritan

May Arkwright Hutton ...... page 38
Mining Camp Cook and Suffragette
1860–1915

Annie Oakley .... page 44
Wild West Show Star
1860–1926

Evelyn Cameron .... page 50
Photographer
1868–1928

Julia Morgan .... page 55
Architect
1872–1957

Willa Cather............. page 63
Author
1873–1947

Georgia O'Keeffe .... page 70
Artist
1887–1986

Further Information .... page 76

Index .... page 77

Where Can I Find It?—Card 1

Index

Numbers in *italics* represent illustrations and photographs.

adoption, 241–242
adventuring, 231–233
Advisory Committee on Women, 242
African Americans, 55–57, 144, 184–187, 202
American West, definition of, 12–13
antislavery movement, 35, 49
architects, 188–191
artists, 51–53, 129–132, 149–152, 165–168
barrel racing, 268–270
Blackfeet Sioux, 27
blackware pottery, 169–171
Buffalo Bill's Wild West Show, 122
buffalo, 63–66, *86*, 87
Cameron, Evelyn, *129*, 129–132
carpentry, 41–42
Cather, Willa, *133*, 133–136
Charbonneau, Jean Baptiste, 15
Cherokee Nation, 178, 209, 254–258

Questions

1. How many pages contain information about the Cherokee Nation?
2. On which pages will you read about the definition of the American West?
3. On which page would you look to find a photograph of Evelyn Cameron?
4. Does this index excerpt support your ideas for a title for this book? Explain why or why not.

Literacy Centers—Take It to Your Seat • EMC 2724 • ©2004 by Evan-Moor Corp.

Table of Contents

Questions

1. What four things are given for each chapter?

2. What can you learn about Julia Morgan from the Table of Contents?

3. What will you find if you turn to page 38?

4. What might be the title of this book?

Index

Numbers in *italics* represent illustrations and photographs.

adoption, 241–242

adventuring, 231–233

Advisory Committee on Women, 242

African Americans, 55–57, 144, 184–187, 202

American West, definition of, 12–13

antislavery movement, 35, 49

architects, 188–191

artists, 51–53, 129–132, 149–152, 165–168

barrel racing, 268–270

Blackfeet Sioux, 27

blackware pottery, 169–171

Buffalo Bill's Wild West Show, 122

buffalo, 63–66, *86*, 87

Cameron, Evelyn, *129*, 129–132

carpentry, 41–42

Cather, Willa, *133*, 133–136

Charbonneau, Jean Baptiste, 15

Cherokee Nation, 178, 209, 254–258

Questions

1. How many pages contain information about the Cherokee Nation?

2. On which pages will you read about the definition of the American West?

3. On which page would you look to find a photograph of Evelyn Cameron?

4. Does this index excerpt support your ideas for a title for this book? Explain why or why not.

   Literacy Centers—Take It to Your Seat • EMC 2724 • ©2004 by Evan-Moor Corp.

Table of Contents

Questions

1. How is this book divided?

2. If you wanted to use descriptive details in your writing, on which page would you begin reading?

3. What will you learn about if you begin reading on page 84?

4. You want to learn more about choosing a name for a character. Should you begin with Chapter 6 or Chapter 7? At what other spot might you start?

Index

alliteration, 9–10, 63

anonymous viewpoint, 35

cause and effect, 98–99

character(s):
 development of, 66–76
 experience and imagination, 56
 growth of, 97–98
 introduction of, 99–100
 names for, 3–5, 61–66
 physical appearance of, 58–61
 and plot, 100–102
 weaknesses of, 69

climax, 101–102

conflict:
 as basis for story, 50–51
 sources of, 51–53

description:
 of characters, 58–61
 selecting words for, 30–31
 of setting, 90–96

details:
 description of, 24–34
 of setting, 90–93

Questions

1. Why are the words indented under *character(s)*?

2. Which pages should you read as you learn to describe the setting of a story?

3. What will you learn about when you read pages 9 and 10?

4. How are topics arranged in an index?

Table of Contents

Questions

1. What is the subject of this book?
2. What will you find if you turn to page 133?
3. How many pages in the book are about racing and kicking games?
4. Besides chapter topics, what other information is referenced in the Table of Contents?

Index

luck and chance, the Indian's viewpoint, 17

markers, for boundaries, 20

Medicine Drum, 137

myth and legend, games in, 16

Obstacle Race, 43

omens, signs, and the effects of dreams on games, 17

Patterns for Partners, 138

Pinecone Hoop Toss, 108

Pole Pull, 140

Rattler!, 70

Ring in a Ring, 147

Shield and Ball, 113

Shield on Shield, 128

singing during guessing games, 157

Sit Pole Pull, 178

Sit Wrestle, 150

Skunk!, 15

Sky Okotoks, 136

Slip Stick, 175

Snow Boat, 173

stalking, 68

staples, 20

Star Ball, 150

Star Groups, 83

Stick and Ring, 183

Stick Relay, 32

Questions

1. Using the Table of Contents and the Index, determine what kind of a game Pinecone Hoop Toss is.

2. Where can you find out about the effects of dreams on games?

3. If you read the information on page 83, will you be reading about a specific game or general information? How do you know?

4. Where would the game Rebound be added to this index?

Table of Contents
Canada

Questions

1. How are chapters indicated in this Table of Contents?

2. What topics will you read about on page 26?

3. What chapter should you read to find information about the different climatic regions in Canada?

4. If you are interested in windsurfing in Canada, what page would you go to?

Index

Factory Theater, Toronto, 173

Fairmont Hot Spring
Resort, B.C., 101

Fairview Cemetery,
Halifax, N.S., 245

Federation du Frog
Lovers (FFL), 39, 192

festivals, 63–65, 267–271

in Alberta, 267, 269

in British Columbia, 68, 93, 267

in Manitoba,129–130, 267, 269

in Newfoundland, 264, 270

in Northwest Territories, 271

Fisgard Lighthouse,
Victoria, B.C., 89

fishing, 46–47, 65, 98, 104, 153

food, 269–270, 274–280

French explorers and
settlers, 11, 126, 133
in Quebec, 202, 208, 210

Questions

1. What is the abbreviation for the Federation du Frog Lovers?

2. Why are some entries in this index capitalized and some lowercased?

3. Where is the Fairview Cemetery located?

4. What pages would have information on festivals in Manitoba?

Word Pictures

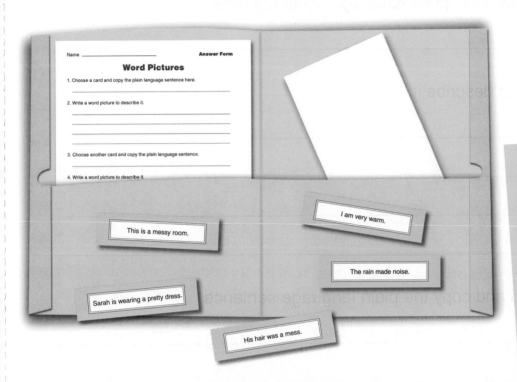

Preparing the Center

1. Prepare a folder following the directions on page 3.

   Cover—page 67
   Student Directions—page 69
   Task Cards—pages 71 and 73

2. Reproduce a supply of the answer form on page 66. Place copies in the left-hand pocket of the folder along with writing paper.

Using the Center

1. The student selects a card that presents a situation or event and writes the plain language sentence on the answer form.

2. The student reads the card and writes a word picture to describe it.

3. The student repeats the task using a second card.

4. On the back of the answer form, the student illustrates one of the word pictures.

Word Pictures

1. Choose a card and copy the plain language sentence here.

_____

2. Write a word picture to describe it.

_____

_____

_____

_____

3. Choose another card and copy the plain language sentence.

_____

4. Write a word picture to describe it.

_____

_____

_____

_____

Bonus: On the back of this form, illustrate one of your sentences.

Word Pictures

A good writer uses colorful, interesting details to help the reader "see" what the writer is describing. These descriptions are **word pictures**.

Plain Language = The ice cream looked good.

Word Picture = My mouth couldn't wait to taste that glorious mound of rich, dark chocolate with puffy chunks of marshmallow, bits of almonds, and a snow-white swirl of whipped cream.

Plain Language = I liked the pretty garden.

Word Picture = Beyond the brilliant rainbows of color and lush green foliage, a bench beckoned me from the cool shade of an elm tree.

Follow these steps:

1. Choose a card and write the plain language sentence on the answer form.

2. Write a word picture to describe the situation or event on the card.

3. Choose one more card and repeat the steps.

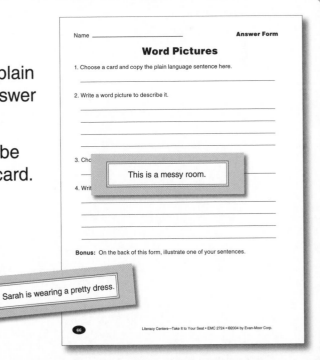

I am very warm.

I like ice cream.

Sarah is wearing a pretty dress.

Jared is cooking dinner.

A bird landed on a limb.

It is raining now.

This is a messy room.

A dog was walking along.

It is a cold day.

I have an old pencil.

I smell pretty flowers.

The tall man is standing.

Word Pictures

EMC 2724
©2004 by Evan-Moor Corp.

Word Pictures

EMC 2724
©2004 by Evan-Moor Corp.

Word Pictures

EMC 2724
©2004 by Evan-Moor Corp.

Word Pictures

EMC 2724
©2004 by Evan-Moor Corp.

Word Pictures

EMC 2724
©2004 by Evan-Moor Corp.

Word Pictures

EMC 2724
©2004 by Evan-Moor Corp.

Word Pictures

EMC 2724
©2004 by Evan-Moor Corp.

Word Pictures

EMC 2724
©2004 by Evan-Moor Corp.

Word Pictures

EMC 2724
©2004 by Evan-Moor Corp.

Word Pictures

EMC 2724
©2004 by Evan-Moor Corp.

Word Pictures

EMC 2724
©2004 by Evan-Moor Corp.

Word Pictures

EMC 2724
©2004 by Evan-Moor Corp.

The rain made noise.

The suitcase was heavy.

The photograph is old.

One boat sits on the lake.

Mary Ester ate the plums.

The sky is clear.

The couch is soft.

The music is loud.

The horse ran along the road.

The pitcher threw the ball.

His hair was a mess.

You look tired.

Word Pictures

EMC 2724
©2004 by Evan-Moor Corp.

Word Pictures

EMC 2724
©2004 by Evan-Moor Corp.

Word Pictures

EMC 2724
©2004 by Evan-Moor Corp.

Word Pictures

EMC 2724
©2004 by Evan-Moor Corp.

Word Pictures

EMC 2724
©2004 by Evan-Moor Corp.

Word Pictures

EMC 2724
©2004 by Evan-Moor Corp.

Word Pictures

EMC 2724
©2004 by Evan-Moor Corp.

Word Pictures

EMC 2724
©2004 by Evan-Moor Corp.

Word Pictures

EMC 2724
©2004 by Evan-Moor Corp.

Word Pictures

EMC 2724
©2004 by Evan-Moor Corp.

Word Pictures

EMC 2724
©2004 by Evan-Moor Corp.

Word Pictures

EMC 2724
©2004 by Evan-Moor Corp.

Groups of Three

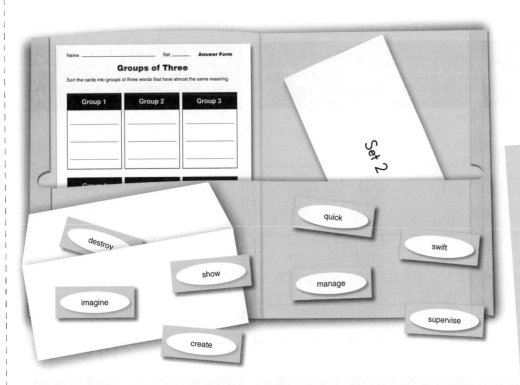

Preparing the Center

1. Prepare a folder following the directions on page 3.

   Cover—page 77
   Student Directions—page 79
   Task Cards—pages 81 and 83

2. Reproduce a supply of the answer form on page 76. Place copies in the left-hand pocket of the folder.

3. Make a dictionary available for students to use.

Using the Center

1. The student selects a set of synonym cards and writes the set number on the answer form.

2. The student sorts the cards into 6 groups of 3 synonyms each.

3. The student copies the words onto the answer form.

Groups of Three

Sort the cards into groups of three words that have almost the same meaning.

Group 1	Group 2	Group 3

Group 4	Group 5	Group 6

Bonus: Think of one more synonym for each group. If you need to, use a dictionary for assistance.

Groups of Three

Synonyms are words that have about the same meaning.

hit—struck

inside—within

damp—moist

Follow these steps:

1. Select one set of cards.

2. Write the set number on the answer form.

3. Match the cards to make groups of three words that are synonyms.

4. Then write each group of synonyms on the answer form.

show	display	exhibit	habit	routine	practice
imagine	invent	create	fair	just	impartial
last	end	final	ruin	spoil	destroy

Groups of Three
Set 1
EMC 2724
©2004 by Evan-Moor Corp.

Groups of Three
Set 1
EMC 2724
©2004 by Evan-Moor Corp.

Groups of Three
Set 1
EMC 2724
©2004 by Evan-Moor Corp.

Groups of Three
Set 1
EMC 2724
©2004 by Evan-Moor Corp.

Groups of Three
Set 1
EMC 2724
©2004 by Evan-Moor Corp.

Groups of Three
Set 1
EMC 2724
©2004 by Evan-Moor Corp.

Groups of Three
Set 1
EMC 2724
©2004 by Evan-Moor Corp.

Groups of Three
Set 1
EMC 2724
©2004 by Evan-Moor Corp.

Groups of Three
Set 1
EMC 2724
©2004 by Evan-Moor Corp.

Groups of Three
Set 1
EMC 2724
©2004 by Evan-Moor Corp.

Groups of Three
Set 1
EMC 2724
©2004 by Evan-Moor Corp.

Groups of Three
Set 1
EMC 2724
©2004 by Evan-Moor Corp.

Groups of Three
Set 1
EMC 2724
©2004 by Evan-Moor Corp.

Groups of Three
Set 1
EMC 2724
©2004 by Evan-Moor Corp.

Groups of Three
Set 1
EMC 2724
©2004 by Evan-Moor Corp.

Groups of Three
Set 1
EMC 2724
©2004 by Evan-Moor Corp.

Groups of Three
Set 1
EMC 2724
©2004 by Evan-Moor Corp.

Groups of Three
Set 1
EMC 2724
©2004 by Evan-Moor Corp.

quick

swift

fleet

rebel

defy

resist

keep

own

retain

tour

trip

excursion

manage

direct

supervise

necessary

needed

required

Groups of Three
Set 2
EMC 2724
©2004 by Evan-Moor Corp.

Groups of Three
Set 2
EMC 2724
©2004 by Evan-Moor Corp.

Groups of Three
Set 2
EMC 2724
©2004 by Evan-Moor Corp.

Groups of Three
Set 2
EMC 2724
©2004 by Evan-Moor Corp.

Groups of Three
Set 2
EMC 2724
©2004 by Evan-Moor Corp.

Groups of Three
Set 2
EMC 2724
©2004 by Evan-Moor Corp.

Groups of Three
Set 2
EMC 2724
©2004 by Evan-Moor Corp.

Groups of Three
Set 2
EMC 2724
©2004 by Evan-Moor Corp.

Groups of Three
Set 2
EMC 2724
©2004 by Evan-Moor Corp.

Groups of Three
Set 2
EMC 2724
©2004 by Evan-Moor Corp.

Groups of Three
Set 2
EMC 2724
©2004 by Evan-Moor Corp.

Groups of Three
Set 2
EMC 2724
©2004 by Evan-Moor Corp.

Groups of Three
Set 2
EMC 2724
©2004 by Evan-Moor Corp.

Groups of Three
Set 2
EMC 2724
©2004 by Evan-Moor Corp.

Groups of Three
Set 2
EMC 2724
©2004 by Evan-Moor Corp.

Groups of Three
Set 2
EMC 2724
©2004 by Evan-Moor Corp.

Just the Opposite

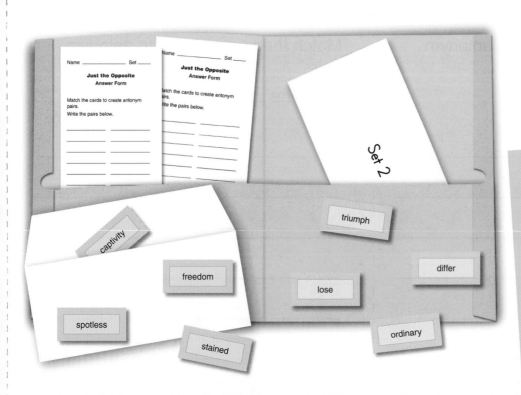

Preparing the Center

1. Prepare a folder following the directions on page 3.

   Cover—page 87
   Student Directions—page 89
   Task Cards—pages 91 and 93

2. Reproduce a supply of the answer form on page 86. Place copies in the left-hand pocket of the folder.

3. Make a dictionary available for students to use.

Using the Center

1. The student selects a set of antonym cards and writes the set number on the answer form.

2. The student matches the antonym cards to create antonym pairs.

3. The student writes the antonym pairs on the answer form.

Name _____ Set ____

Name _____ Set ____

Just the Opposite
Answer Form

Match the cards to create antonym pairs.

Write the pairs below.

_____ _____

_____ _____

_____ _____

_____ _____

_____ _____

_____ _____

_____ _____

_____ _____

_____ _____

_____ _____

Bonus: On the back of this form, write two or more antonym pairs. Write a sentence that includes a pair of antonyms.

Example: The weather changed from *hot* to *cold.*

Just the Opposite
Answer Form

Match the cards to create antonym pairs.

Write the pairs below.

_____ _____

_____ _____

_____ _____

_____ _____

_____ _____

_____ _____

_____ _____

_____ _____

_____ _____

_____ _____

Bonus: On the back of this form, write two or more antonym pairs. Write a sentence that includes a pair of antonyms.

Example: The weather changed from *hot* to *cold.*

Just the Opposite

Antonyms are words that have opposite meanings.

smooth—bumpy

find—lose

object—agree

Follow these steps:

1. Select one set of cards.

2. Write the set number on the answer form.

3. Match the cards to make antonym pairs.

4. Then write the antonym pairs on the answer form.

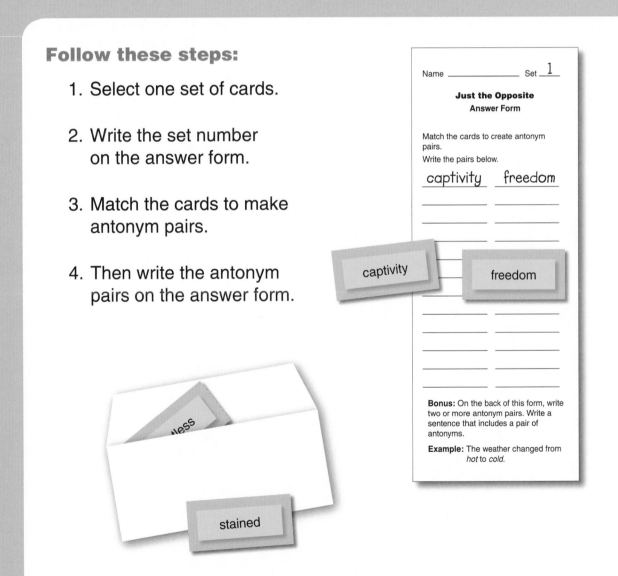

Name _____ Set 1

Just the Opposite
Answer Form

Match the cards to create antonym pairs.
Write the pairs below.

captivity   freedom
_____ _____
_____ _____
_____ _____

captivity   freedom

_____ _____
_____ _____
_____ _____
_____ _____

Bonus: On the back of this form, write two or more antonym pairs. Write a sentence that includes a pair of antonyms.

Example: The weather changed from *hot* to *cold*.

stained

captivity	freedom	careful
haphazard	spotless	stained
rapid	slow	employed
jobless	cautious	daring
rigid	flexible	saturated
dry	restrain	release
humble	conceited	doubtful
confident	serious	comical

Just the Opposite
Set 1

EMC 2724
©2004 by Evan-Moor Corp.

Just the Opposite
Set 1

EMC 2724
©2004 by Evan-Moor Corp.

Just the Opposite
Set 1

EMC 2724
©2004 by Evan-Moor Corp.

Just the Opposite
Set 1

EMC 2724
©2004 by Evan-Moor Corp.

Just the Opposite
Set 1

EMC 2724
©2004 by Evan-Moor Corp.

Just the Opposite
Set 1

EMC 2724
©2004 by Evan-Moor Corp.

Just the Opposite
Set 1

EMC 2724
©2004 by Evan-Moor Corp.

Just the Opposite
Set 1

EMC 2724
©2004 by Evan-Moor Corp.

Just the Opposite
Set 1

EMC 2724
©2004 by Evan-Moor Corp.

Just the Opposite
Set 1

EMC 2724
©2004 by Evan-Moor Corp.

Just the Opposite
Set 1

EMC 2724
©2004 by Evan-Moor Corp.

Just the Opposite
Set 1

EMC 2724
©2004 by Evan-Moor Corp.

Just the Opposite
Set 1

EMC 2724
©2004 by Evan-Moor Corp.

Just the Opposite
Set 1

EMC 2724
©2004 by Evan-Moor Corp.

Just the Opposite
Set 1

EMC 2724
©2004 by Evan-Moor Corp.

Just the Opposite
Set 1

EMC 2724
©2004 by Evan-Moor Corp.

Just the Opposite
Set 1

EMC 2724
©2004 by Evan-Moor Corp.

Just the Opposite
Set 1

EMC 2724
©2004 by Evan-Moor Corp.

Just the Opposite
Set 1

EMC 2724
©2004 by Evan-Moor Corp.

Just the Opposite
Set 1

EMC 2724
©2004 by Evan-Moor Corp.

Just the Opposite
Set 1

EMC 2724
©2004 by Evan-Moor Corp.

Just the Opposite
Set 1

EMC 2724
©2004 by Evan-Moor Corp.

Just the Opposite
Set 1

EMC 2724
©2004 by Evan-Moor Corp.

Just the Opposite
Set 1

EMC 2724
©2004 by Evan-Moor Corp.

fail	triumph	match
differ	stout	slender
ordinary	uncommon	preserve
waste	encourage	deter
retrieve	lose	bellow
whisper	capture	release
friendly	grouchy	tangle
unravel	durable	fragile

Just the Opposite
Set 2

EMC 2724
©2004 by Evan-Moor Corp.

Just the Opposite
Set 2

EMC 2724
©2004 by Evan-Moor Corp.

Just the Opposite
Set 2

EMC 2724
©2004 by Evan-Moor Corp.

Just the Opposite
Set 2

EMC 2724
©2004 by Evan-Moor Corp.

Just the Opposite
Set 2

EMC 2724
©2004 by Evan-Moor Corp.

Just the Opposite
Set 2

EMC 2724
©2004 by Evan-Moor Corp.

Just the Opposite
Set 2

EMC 2724
©2004 by Evan-Moor Corp.

Just the Opposite
Set 2

EMC 2724
©2004 by Evan-Moor Corp.

Just the Opposite
Set 2

EMC 2724
©2004 by Evan-Moor Corp.

Just the Opposite
Set 2

EMC 2724
©2004 by Evan-Moor Corp.

Just the Opposite
Set 2

EMC 2724
©2004 by Evan-Moor Corp.

Just the Opposite
Set 2

EMC 2724
©2004 by Evan-Moor Corp.

Just the Opposite
Set 2

EMC 2724
©2004 by Evan-Moor Corp.

Just the Opposite
Set 2

EMC 2724
©2004 by Evan-Moor Corp.

Just the Opposite
Set 2

EMC 2724
©2004 by Evan-Moor Corp.

Just the Opposite
Set 2

EMC 2724
©2004 by Evan-Moor Corp.

Just the Opposite
Set 2

EMC 2724
©2004 by Evan-Moor Corp.

Just the Opposite
Set 2

EMC 2724
©2004 by Evan-Moor Corp.

Just the Opposite
Set 2

EMC 2724
©2004 by Evan-Moor Corp.

Just the Opposite
Set 2

EMC 2724
©2004 by Evan-Moor Corp.

Just the Opposite
Set 2

EMC 2724
©2004 by Evan-Moor Corp.

Just the Opposite
Set 2

EMC 2724
©2004 by Evan-Moor Corp.

Just the Opposite
Set 2

EMC 2724
©2004 by Evan-Moor Corp.

Just the Opposite
Set 2

EMC 2724
©2004 by Evan-Moor Corp.

What's an Idiom?

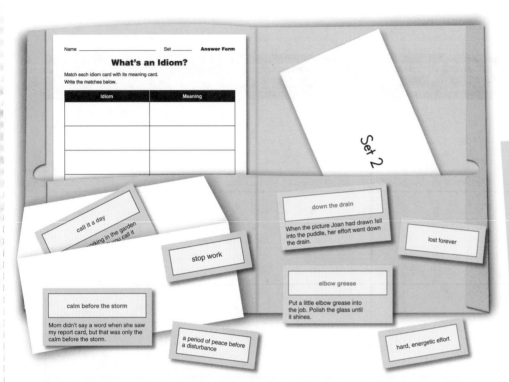

Preparing the Center

1. Prepare a folder following the directions on page 3.

   Cover—page 97
   Student Directions—page 99
   Task Cards—pages 101–105

2. Reproduce a supply of the answer form on page 96. Place copies in the left-hand pocket of the folder.

3. Place the idiom cards for Set 1 in a bag or envelope. Place the meaning cards in a bag or envelope. Label the bags or envelopes with the set number.

4. Repeat for Set 2.

Using the Center

1. The student selects a set of idiom and meaning cards and writes the set number on the answer form.

2. The student reads an idiom card and chooses the meaning card that matches the idiom card.

3. The student continues until all cards have been matched.

4. The student records the matches on the answer form.

What's an Idiom?

Match each idiom card with its meaning card.

Write the matches below.

Idiom	Meaning

Bonus: Select one idiom card. On the back of this form, draw a picture to show the literal meaning—what the words seem to be saying. For example, if you illustrated an idiom card with the sentence *The two brothers, Scott and Josh, are like two peas in a pod,* you might draw a giant pod with two boys in it.

Scott and Josh are like two peas in a pod.

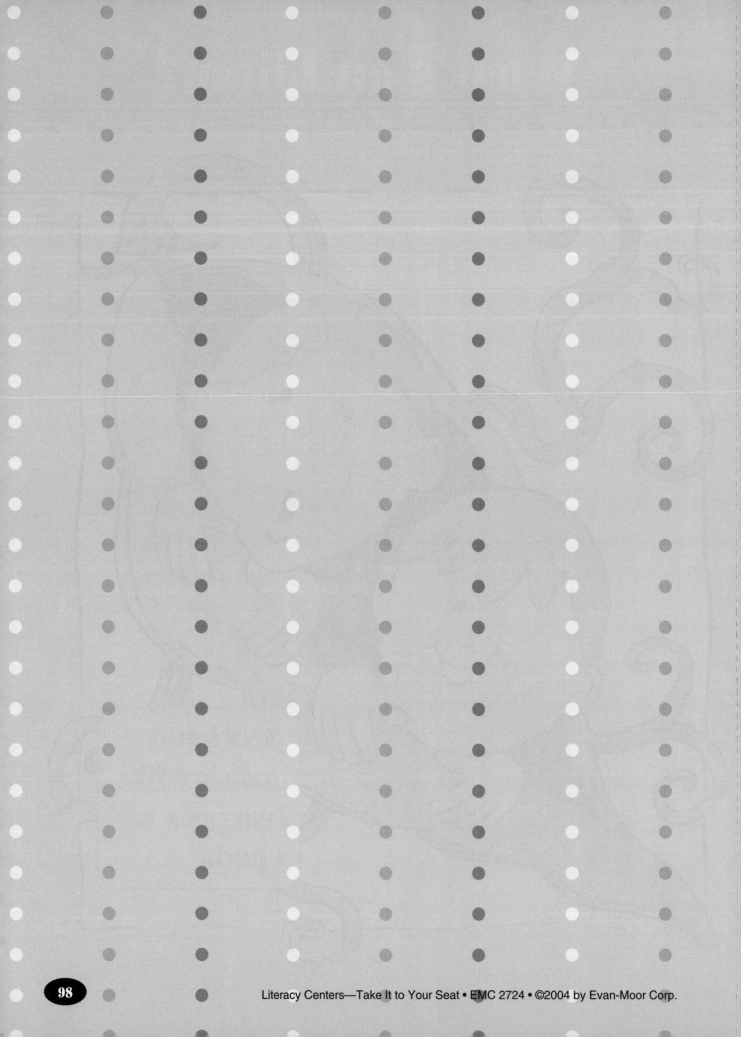

What's an Idiom?

An **idiom** is a phrase with a special meaning. The meaning of the phrase has little, often nothing, to do with the meanings of the words taken one by one.

The idiom ***let the cat out of the bag*** means to reveal a secret.

Follow these steps:

1. Take an answer form and a set of task cards. Write the set number on the answer form.

2. Select an idiom card.

3. Find a meaning card that matches the idiom card.

4. Match all the cards.

5. Write your matches on the answer form.

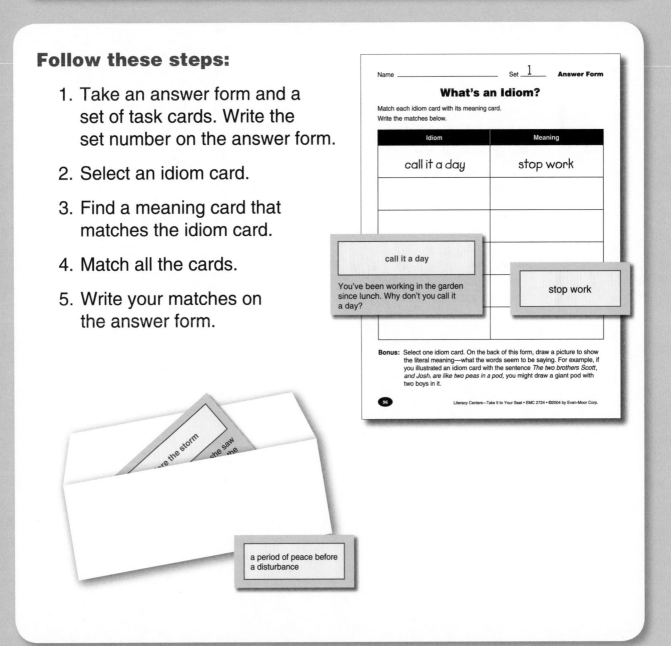

by the skin of your teeth

Chelsea jumped off the rock just as it came loose and escaped injury by the skin of her teeth.

butterflies in the stomach

I can't give a speech without getting butterflies in my stomach.

button your lip

Josh talked about his camping trip so much that we finally told him to button his lip.

call it a day

You've been working in the garden since lunch. Why don't you call it a day?

calm before the storm

Mom didn't say a word when she saw my report card, but that was only the calm before the storm.

can't see the forest for the trees

My teacher sees all my misspellings, but she misses the point of my essay. She can't see the forest for the trees.

What's an Idiom?
Idiom Card
Set 1

What's an Idiom?
Idiom Card
Set 1

What's an Idiom?
Idiom Card
Set 1

What's an Idiom?
Idiom Card
Set 1

What's an Idiom?
Idiom Card
Set 1

What's an Idiom?
Idiom Card
Set 1

make ends meet	miss the boat	carry the ball
On his salary, Mr. Peet can hardly make ends meet.	If you don't sign up for the team, you'll miss the boat for summer soccer.	As for organizing the student council picnic, Brad will carry the ball.
down the drain	elbow grease	scratch the surface
When the picture Joan had drawn fell into the puddle, her effort went down the drain.	Put a little elbow grease into the job. Polish the glass until it shines.	I have written the first chapter of my ten-chapter report, but I have barely scratched the surface.

What's an Idiom?
Idiom Card
Set 2

What's an Idiom?
Idiom Card
Set 2

What's an Idiom?
Idiom Card
Set 2

What's an Idiom?
Idiom Card
Set 2

What's an Idiom?
Idiom Card
Set 2

What's an Idiom?
Idiom Card
Set 2

just barely	earn just enough to live
a fluttering feeling in the stomach usually caused by nervousness	lose an opportunity
be quiet	make sure the job gets done right
stop work	lost forever
a period of peace before a disturbance	hard, energetic effort
to be so involved in details that you miss the whole picture	to deal with only a very small part of a subject

What's an Idiom?

Meaning Card

Set 2

EMC 2724 • ©2004 by Evan-Moor Corp.

What's an Idiom?

Meaning Card

Set 1

EMC 272 • ©2004 by Evan-Moor Corp.

What's an Idiom?

Meaning Card

Set 2

EMC 2724 • ©2004 by Evan-Moor Corp.

What's an Idiom?

Meaning Card

Set 1

EMC 272 • ©2004 by Evan-Moor Corp.

What's an Idiom?

Meaning Card

Set 2

EMC 2724 • ©2004 by Evan-Moor Corp.

What's an Idiom?

Meaning Card

Set 1

EMC 272 • ©2004 by Evan-Moor Corp.

What's an Idiom?

Meaning Card

Set 2

EMC 2724 • ©2004 by Evan-Moor Corp.

What's an Idiom?

Meaning Card

Set 1

EMC 272 • ©2004 by Evan-Moor Corp.

What's an Idiom?

Meaning Card

Set 2

EMC 2724 • ©2004 by Evan-Moor Corp.

What's an Idiom?

Meaning Card

Set 1

EMC 272 • ©2004 by Evan-Moor Corp.

What's an Idiom?

Meaning Card

Set 2

EMC 2724 • ©2004 by Evan-Moor Corp.

What's an Idiom?

Meaning Card

Set 1

EMC 272 • ©2004 by Evan-Moor Corp.

Two into One

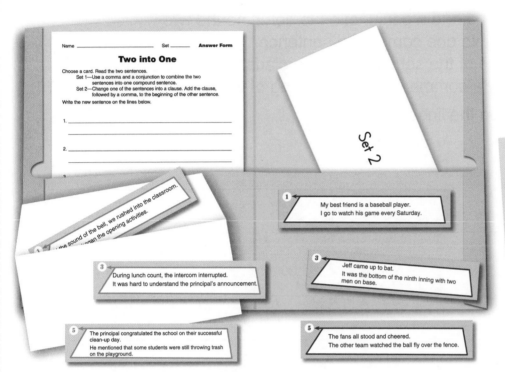

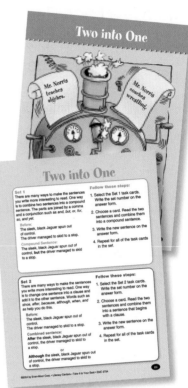

Preparing the Center

1. Prepare a folder following the directions on page 3.

   Cover—page 109
   Student Directions—page 111
   Task Cards—pages 113 and 115

2. Reproduce a supply of the answer form on page 108. Place copies in the left-hand pocket of the folder.

Using the Center

1. The student selects a set of task cards and writes the set number on the answer form.

2. The student chooses a task card, reads the two sentences, and combines them into one sentence.

   Set 1: The student uses a conjunction and a comma to combine the two sentences into a compound sentence.

   Set 2: The student changes one of the sentences into a dependent clause and adds the clause to the beginning of the other sentence.

3. The student writes the new sentences on the answer form.

Two into One

Choose a card. Read the two sentences.

  Set 1—Use a comma and a conjunction to combine the two
    sentences into one compound sentence.
  Set 2—Change one of the sentences into a clause. Add the clause,
    followed by a comma, to the beginning of the other sentence.

Write the new sentence on the lines below.

1. _____

   _____

2. _____

   _____

3. _____

   _____

4. _____

   _____

5. _____

   _____

6. _____

   _____

Two into One

Two into One

Set 1

There are many ways to make the sentences you write more interesting to read. One way is to combine two sentences into a compound sentence. The parts are joined by a comma and a conjunction such as *and, but, or, for, so,* and *yet.*

Before:
The sleek, black Jaguar spun out of control.
The driver managed to skid to a stop.

Compound Sentence:
The sleek, black Jaguar spun out of control, **but** the driver managed to skid to a stop.

Follow these steps:

1. Select the Set 1 task cards. Write the set number on the answer form.

2. Choose a card. Read the two sentences and combine them into a compound sentence.

3. Write the new sentence on the answer form.

4. Repeat for all of the task cards in the set.

Set 2

There are many ways to make the sentences you write more interesting to read. One way is to change one sentence into a clause and add it to the other sentence. Words such as *since, after, because, although, when,* and *as* help you do this.

Before:
The sleek, black Jaguar spun out of control.
The driver managed to skid to a stop.

Combined sentence:
After the sleek, black Jaguar spun out of control, the driver managed to skid to a stop.

or

Although the sleek, black Jaguar spun out of control, the driver managed to skid to a stop.

Follow these steps:

1. Select the Set 2 task cards. Write the set number on the answer form.

2. Choose a card. Read the two sentences and combine them into a sentence that begins with a clause.

3. Write the new sentence on the answer form.

4. Repeat for all of the task cards in the set.

1 At the sound of the bell, we rushed into the classroom.
Miss Bush began the opening activities.

2 She usually begins by taking roll.
Today, she took the lunch count first.

3 During lunch count, the intercom interrupted.
It was hard to understand the principal's announcement.

4 We asked what the principal had said.
Miss Bush called the office.

5 The principal congratulated the school on their successful clean-up day.
He mentioned that some students were still throwing trash on the playground.

6 Finally, the opening activities were over.
We could begin our work.

Two into One
Set 1

EMC 2724 • ©2004 by Evan-Moor Corp.

Two into One
Set 1

EMC 2724 • ©2004 by Evan-Moor Corp.

Two into One
Set 1

EMC 2724 • ©2004 by Evan-Moor Corp.

Two into One
Set 1

EMC 2724 • ©2004 by Evan-Moor Corp.

Two into One
Set 1

EMC 2724 • ©2004 by Evan-Moor Corp.

Two into One
Set 1

EMC 2724 • ©2004 by Evan-Moor Corp.

1 My best friend is a baseball player.
I go to watch his game every Saturday.

2 Jeff has a good batting average.
He hits clean-up for the Hot Shots.

3 Jeff came up to bat.
It was the bottom of the ninth inning with two men on base.

4 He missed the first two pitches.
He connected on the third pitch.

5 The fans all stood and cheered.
The other team watched the ball fly over the fence.

6 His homerun drove in two runs.
Jeff's team won the game.

Two into One
Set 2

EMC 2724 • ©2004 by Evan-Moor Corp.

Two into One
Set 2

EMC 2724 • ©2004 by Evan-Moor Corp.

Two into One
Set 2

EMC 2724 • ©2004 by Evan-Moor Corp.

Two into One
Set 2

EMC 2724 • ©2004 by Evan-Moor Corp.

Two into One
Set 2

EMC 2724 • ©2004 by Evan-Moor Corp.

Two into One
Set 2

EMC 2724 • ©2004 by Evan-Moor Corp.

Fix It Up!

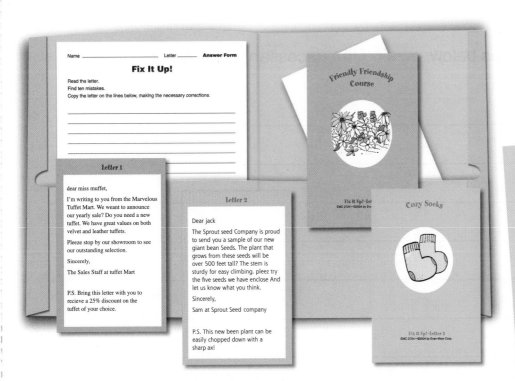

Preparing the Center

1. Prepare a folder following the directions on page 3.

   Cover—page 119
   Student Directions—page 121
   Task Cards—pages 123–127

2. Reproduce a supply of the answer form on page 118. Place copies in the left-hand pocket of the folder.

Using the Center

1. The student selects a task card and writes the letter number on the answer form.

2. The student reads the letter and finds ten errors.

3. The student copies the letter onto the answer form, making the necessary corrections.

Fix It Up!

Read the letter.

Find ten mistakes.

Copy the letter on the lines below, making the necessary corrections.

_____

_____

_____

_____

_____

_____

_____

_____

_____

_____

_____

_____

_____

_____

Bonus: On the back of this form, write a reply to the letter.

Fix It Up!

Fix It Up!

Dear Mother Goose:

We are pleased to inform you that your book of rhymes has been selected for the silliest book award!

Congratulations,

Silly Inc.

Follow these steps:

1. Select one task card. Write the letter number on the answer form.

2. Read the letter.

3. Find ten mistakes.

4. Copy the letter onto the answer form, making the necessary corrections.

Name _____ Letter _____ **Answer Form**

Fix It Up!

Read the letter.
Find ten mistakes.
Copy the letter on the lines below, making the necessary corrections.

_____

_____

_____

_____

_____

_____

_____

_____

_____

_____

_____

_____

_____

a reply to the letter.

Take It to Your Seat • EMC 2724 • ©2004 by Evan-Moor Corp.

Letter 2

Dear jack

The Sprout seed Company is proud to send you a sample of our new giant bean Seeds. The plant that grows from these seeds will be over 500 feet tall? The stem is sturdy for easy climbing. pleez try the five seeds we have enclose And let us know what you think.

Sincerely,

Sam at Sprout Seed Company

P.S. This new been plant can be easily chopped down with a sh ax!

Sprout Seed Company

Fix It Up!—Letter 1
EMC 2724 • ©2004 by Evan-Moor Corp.

Letter 2

Dear jack

The Sprout seed Company is proud to send you a sample of our new giant bean Seeds. The plant that grows from these seeds will be over 500 feet tall? The stem is sturdy for easy climbing. pleez try the five seeds we have enclose And let us know what you think.

Sincerely,

Sam at Sprout Seed company

P.S. This new been plant can be easily chopped down with a sharp ax!

Letter 1

dear miss muffet,

I'm writing to you from the Marvelous Tuffet Mart. We weant to announce our yearly sale? Do you need a new tuffet. We have great values on both velvet and leather tuffets.

Pleeze stop by our showroom to see our outstanding selection.

Sincerely

The Sales Staff at tuffet Mart

P.S. Bring this letter with you to recieve a 25% discount on the tuffet of your choice.

Sprout Seed Company

Fix It Up!-Letter 2
EMC 2724 • ©2004 by Evan-Moor Corp.

Marvelous Tuffet Mart

Fix It Up!-Letter 1
EMC 2724 • ©2004 by Evan-Moor Corp.

Letter 4

dear mary-mary

I understand that you are quite contrary. You may want to consider enrollin in one of our freindship classes. Even the most grumpy characters have made lasting friendships after attending our classes. I have enclosed the july schedule for your information

sincerely,

Professor Get-a-long Great

P.S. Enroll today and receive $200 off the cost of your class?

Letter 3

Dear john

Enclosed you will find a pear of our cozy sleep socks. Please try them and let us know whether you find them helpful. with or without shoes, they will keep your feet cozy and warm You may purchase additional pairs at you local department store?

yours truely

The Sleep Staff at cozysocks.com

P.S. Additional socks are available online at **www.cozysocks.com.**

Friendly Friendship Course

Fix It Up!–Letter 4
EMC 2724 • ©2004 by Evan-Moor Corp.

Cozy Socks

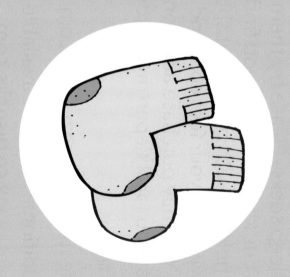

Fix It Up!–Letter 3
EMC 2724 • ©2004 by Evan-Moor Corp.

Dear little pigs

We r sending you a free sample of our house plans? Next time you build a new home, follow the easy steps. Your house will be strong and you will be safe.

Sincerely

master Builders

P.s. Buy your building supplies at our warehouse. We have bricks sticks, and straw.

dear little Boy Blue

Congratulations! you have one a set of horn lessons. soon you will be blowing you're favorite tunes! Call today to set up your first lesson.

yours truly,

mr Music

P.S. We have a great selection of music books, too.

Master Builders

Fix It Up!–Letter 6
EMC 2724 • ©2004 by Evan-Moor Corp.

Music Lesson Masters

Fix It Up!–Letter 5
EMC 2724 • ©2004 by Evan-Moor Corp.

Pattern a Poem

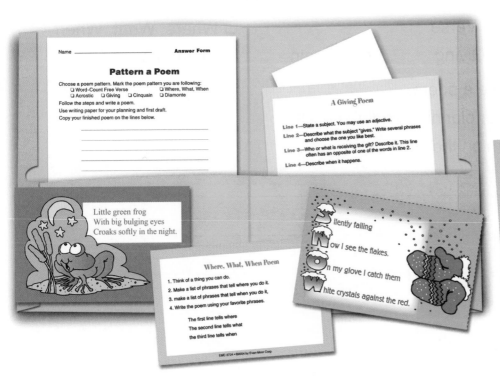

Preparing the Center

1. Prepare a folder following the directions on page 3.

   Cover—page 131
   Student Directions—page 133
   Task Cards—pages 135–139

2. Reproduce a supply of the answer form on page 130. Place copies in the left-hand pocket of the folder along with additional writing paper.

Using the Center

1. The student selects a poem pattern card, takes an answer form, and marks the poem pattern on the answer form.

2. The student writes an original poem following the pattern.

3. The student copies the poem onto the answer form.

Pattern a Poem

Choose a poem pattern. Mark the poem pattern you are following:

❏ Word-Count Free Verse   ❏ Where, What, When

❏ Acrostic   ❏ Giving   ❏ Cinquain   ❏ Diamonte

Follow the steps and write a poem.

Use writing paper for your planning and first draft.

Copy your finished poem on the lines below.

_____

_____

_____

_____

_____

_____

_____

_____

_____

_____

Bonus: Decorate this form with colorful borders or pictures.

Pattern a Poem

Acrostic Poem

Giving Poem

Cinquain

Diamonte

Free Verse

Where, What, When Poem

Pattern a Poem

Each card has a poem on it. Each poem follows a different pattern. You will write your own poem, following one of the patterns.

Follow these steps:

1. Take the task cards and an answer form.

2. Read the poems. Choose your favorite.

3. Turn over the card to see the pattern of the poem.

4. Mark the pattern on your answer form.

5. Follow the steps to write your own poem. Write your first draft on plain writing paper.

6. Reread your poem. Make sure you followed the instructions for each line. Write your final draft on the answer form.

Name _____   Answer Form

Pattern a Poem

Choose a poem pattern. Mark the poem pattern you are following:
☐ Word-Count Free Verse   ☐ Where, What, When
☐ Acrostic   ☐ Giving   ☐ Cinquain   ☐ Diamonte
Follow the steps and write a poem.
Use writing paper for your planning and first draft.
Copy your finished poem on the lines below.

by Evan-Moor Corp.

Little green frog
With big bulging eyes
Croaks softly in the night.

Word-Count Free Verse

1. Choose an animal.

2. Think about how the animal looks. List the words that tell about its looks on some writing paper.

3. Think about how the animal sounds. List the words that tell about its sounds.

4. Write about your animal.

   3 words—Name the animal.

   4 words—Tell how it looks.

   5 words—Tell how it sounds.

EMC 2724 •©2004 by Evan-Moor Corp.

Little green frog
With big bulging eyes
Croaks softly in the night.

Under the big elm tree,

The juice drips down my chin

As I take a giant bite of watermelon.

Word-Count Free Verse

1. Choose an animal.

2. Think about how the animal looks. List the words that tell about its looks on some writing paper.

3. Think about how the animal sounds. List the words that tell about its sounds.

4. Write about your animal.

    3 words—Name the animal.

    4 words—Tell how it looks.

    5 words—Tell how it sounds.

Where, What, When Poem

1. Think of a thing you can do.
2. Make a list of phrases that tell where you do it.
3. Make a list of phrases that tell when you do it.
4. Write the poem using your favorite phrases.

    The first line tells where.

    The second line tells what.

    The third line tells when.

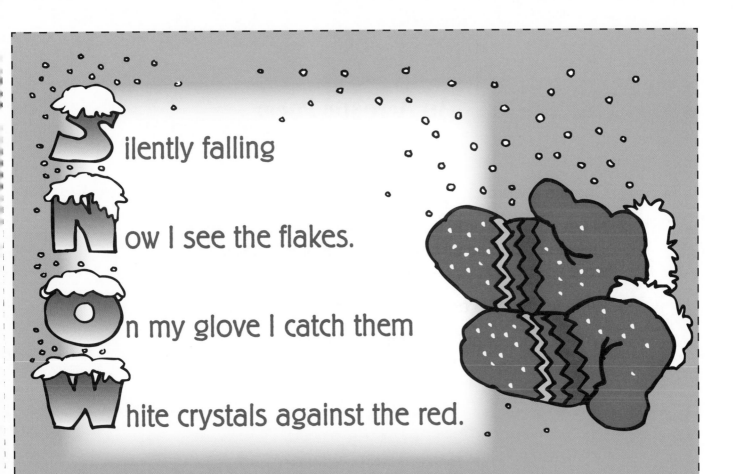

Silently falling

Now I see the flakes.

On my glove I catch them

White crystals against the red.

Libraries
give answers
to eager, questioning minds
whenever they are asked.

An Acrostic Poem

1. Choose a word.

2. Make a list of words that tell about the word you picked. The words should all begin with one of the letters in the word you chose.

3. Write your word vertically. Make the letters dark.

4. Write a word or phrase after each letter.

A Giving Poem

Line 1—State a subject. You may use an adjective.

Line 2—Describe what the subject "gives." Write several phrases and choose the one you like best.

Line 3—Who or what is receiving the gift? Describe it. This line often has an opposite of one of the words in line 2.

Line 4—Describe when it happens.

Kitten
Curious, sweet
Exploring, purring, napping
Velvet in my lap
Meow

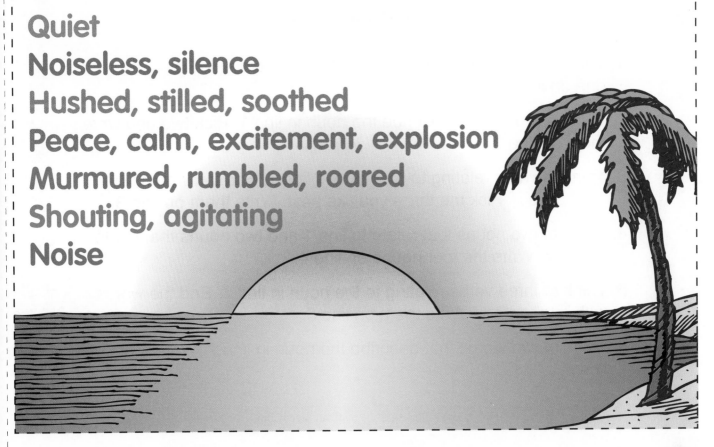

Quiet
Noiseless, silence
Hushed, stilled, soothed
Peace, calm, excitement, explosion
Murmured, rumbled, roared
Shouting, agitating
Noise

A Cinquain

1. Write a one-word subject.

2. Use two adjectives to describe the subject.

3. Write three descriptive action words about the subject.

4. Make a short statement about the subject—usually four words.

5. End with one word—often a synonym for the subject.

A Diamonte

1. Think of two nouns that are opposites. Write one on line 1 and one on line 7.

2. Think of words that describe the noun in line 1. Pick two and write them on line 2.

3. Think of verbs relating to the noun in line 1. End the words with "ing" or "ed." Pick the three you like best. Write them on line 3.

4. Think of two nouns that relate to line 1 and two nouns that relate to line 7. Write the four nouns on line 4.

5. Think of three verbs relating to the noun in line 7. End the words with "ing" or "ed." Write them on line 5.

6. Think of two words that describe the noun in line 7. Write them on line 6.

Get to the Root of It

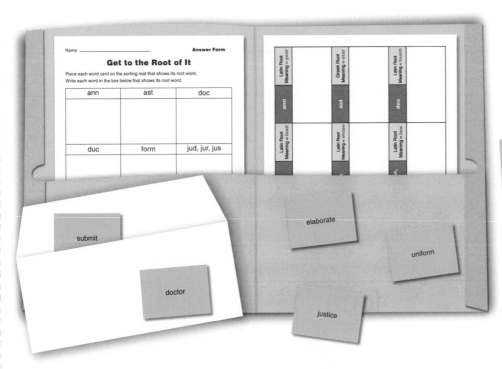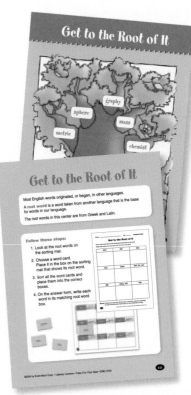

Preparing the Center

1. Prepare a folder following the directions on page 3.

   Cover—page 143
   Student Directions—page 145
   Sorting Mat—page 147
   Task Cards—pages 149 and 151

2. Reproduce a supply of the answer form on page 142. Place copies in the left-hand pocket of the folder.

3. Make a dictionary available for students to use.

Using the Center

1. The student selects the word cards and an answer form.

2. On the sorting mat, the student matches each word card to its root word by placing the card in its correct box.

3. On the answer form, the student writes each word under its root, just as he or she classified the word on the sorting mat.

Get to the Root of It

Place each word card on the sorting mat that shows its root word.

Write each word in the box below that shows its root word.

ann	ast	doc
duc	**form**	**jud, jur, jus**
lab	**miss, mit**	**vac**

Bonus: Choose one root word. On the back of this form, write the meanings
for each word that came from that root. Use a dictionary to help.

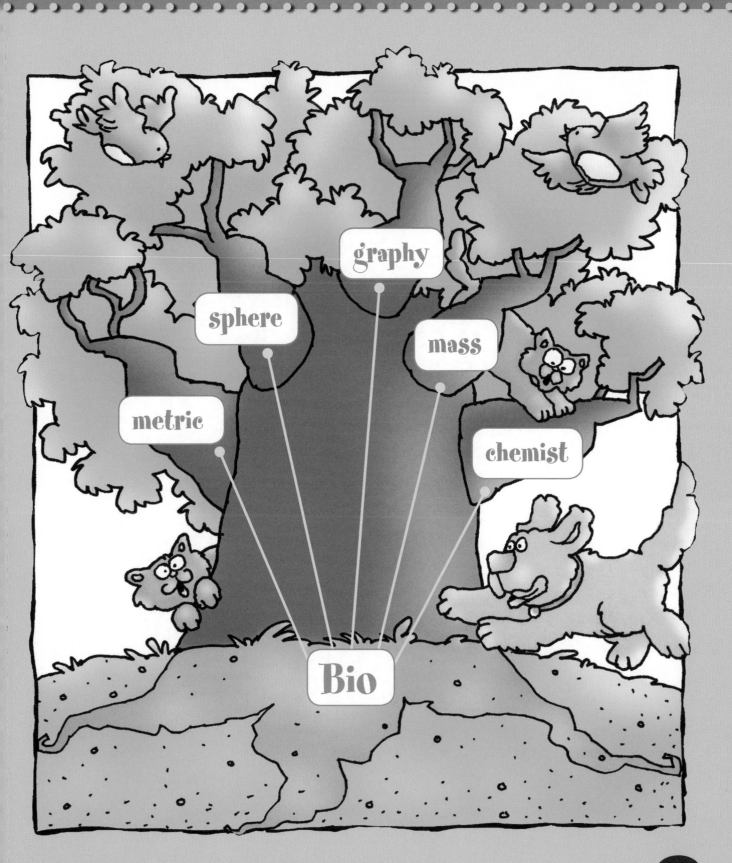

Get to the Root of It

Most English words originated, or began, in other languages.

A **root word** is a word taken from another language that is the base for words in our language.

The root words in this center are from Greek and Latin.

Follow these steps:

1. Look at the root words on the sorting mat.

2. Choose a word card. Place it in the box on the sorting mat that shows its root word.

3. Sort all the word cards and place them in the correct boxes.

4. On the answer form, write each word in its matching root word box.

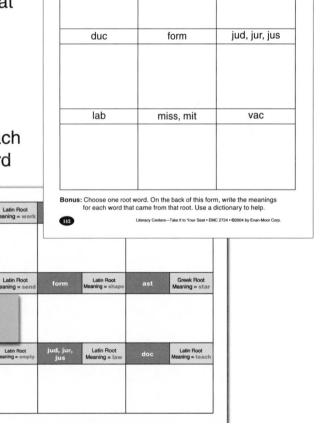

Name _____   Answer Form

Get to the Root of It

Place each word card on the sorting mat that shows its root word.
Write each word in the box below that shows its root word.

ann	ast	doc
duc	form	jud, jur, jus
lab	miss, mit	vac

Bonus: Choose one root word. On the back of this form, write the meanings for each word that came from that root. Use a dictionary to help.

142

Literacy Centers—Take It to Your Seat • EMC 2724 • ©2004 by Evan-Moor Corp.

ann	Latin Root Meaning = year
ast	Greek Root Meaning = star
doc	Latin Root Meaning = teach
duc	Latin Root Meaning = lead
form	Latin Root Meaning = shape
jud, jur, jus	Latin Root Meaning = law
lab	Latin Root Meaning = work
miss, mit	Latin Root Meaning = send
vac	Latin Root Meaning = empty

Get to the Root of It
Sorting Mat

vacuum	doctor	uniform	submit
formal	document	transform	elaborate
annual	duct	justice	missile
astronaut	aqueduct	labor	vacation

Get to the Root of It
Word Card
EMC 2724
©2004 by Evan-Moor Corp.

Get to the Root of It
Word Card
EMC 2724
©2004 by Evan-Moor Corp.

Get to the Root of It
Word Card
EMC 2724
©2004 by Evan-Moor Corp.

Get to the Root of It
Word Card
EMC 2724
©2004 by Evan-Moor Corp.

Get to the Root of It
Word Card
EMC 2724
©2004 by Evan-Moor Corp.

Get to the Root of It
Word Card
EMC 2724
©2004 by Evan-Moor Corp.

Get to the Root of It
Word Card
EMC 2724
©2004 by Evan-Moor Corp.

Get to the Root of It
Word Card
EMC 2724
©2004 by Evan-Moor Corp.

Get to the Root of It
Word Card
EMC 2724
©2004 by Evan-Moor Corp.

Get to the Root of It
Word Card
EMC 2724
©2004 by Evan-Moor Corp.

Get to the Root of It
Word Card
EMC 2724
©2004 by Evan-Moor Corp.

Get to the Root of It
Word Card
EMC 2724
©2004 by Evan-Moor Corp.

Get to the Root of It
Word Card
EMC 2724
©2004 by Evan-Moor Corp.

Get to the Root of It
Word Card
EMC 2724
©2004 by Evan-Moor Corp.

Get to the Root of It
Word Card
EMC 2724
©2004 by Evan-Moor Corp.

reform	judge	astronomy	doctrine
jury	asterisk	disaster	conduct
educate	anniversary	annuity	laboratory
remit	dismiss	vacant	evacuate

Get to the Root of It
Word Card
©2004 by Evan-Moor Corp.
EMC 2724

Get to the Root of It
Word Card
©2004 by Evan-Moor Corp.
EMC 2724

Get to the Root of It
Word Card
©2004 by Evan-Moor Corp.
EMC 2724

Get to the Root of It
Word Card
©2004 by Evan-Moor Corp.
EMC 2724

Get to the Root of It
Word Card
©2004 by Evan-Moor Corp.
EMC 2724

Get to the Root of It
Word Card
©2004 by Evan-Moor Corp.
EMC 2724

Get to the Root of It
Word Card
©2004 by Evan-Moor Corp.
EMC 2724

Get to the Root of It
Word Card
©2004 by Evan-Moor Corp.
EMC 2724

Get to the Root of It
Word Card
©2004 by Evan-Moor Corp.
EMC 2724

Get to the Root of It
Word Card
©2004 by Evan-Moor Corp.
EMC 2724

Get to the Root of It
Word Card
©2004 by Evan-Moor Corp.
EMC 2724

Get to the Root of It
Word Card
©2004 by Evan-Moor Corp.
EMC 2724

Get to the Root of It
Word Card
©2004 by Evan-Moor Corp.
EMC 2724

Get to the Root of It
Word Card
©2004 by Evan-Moor Corp.
EMC 2724

Get to the Root of It
Word Card
©2004 by Evan-Moor Corp.
EMC 2724

Get to the Root of It
Word Card
©2004 by Evan-Moor Corp.
EMC 2724

Here's How to Do It!

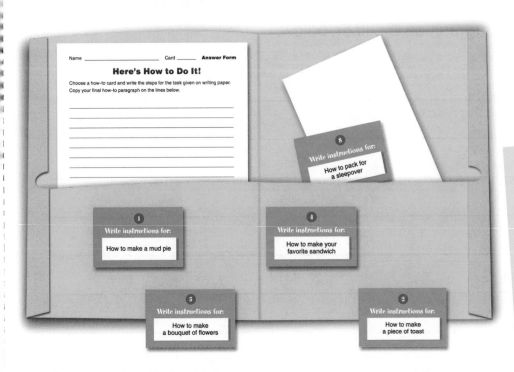

Preparing the Center

1. Prepare a folder following the directions on page 3.

   Cover—page 155
   Student Directions—page 157
   Task Cards—pages 159 and 161

2. Reproduce a supply of the answer form on page 154. Place copies in the left-hand pocket of the folder along with writing paper.

Using the Center

1. The student selects a how-to card and an answer form, and writes the card number on the answer form.

2. The student writes a step-by-step list that gives directions for the task on the card.

3. The student writes a how-to paragraph using the list as reference.

4. The student corrects and copies his or her paragraph onto the answer form.

Here's How to Do It!

Choose a how-to card and write the steps for the task given on writing paper.
Copy your final how-to paragraph on the lines below.

_____

_____

_____

_____

_____

_____

_____

_____

_____

_____

_____

_____

_____

Bonus: Draw small pictures to illustrate each step in the process.

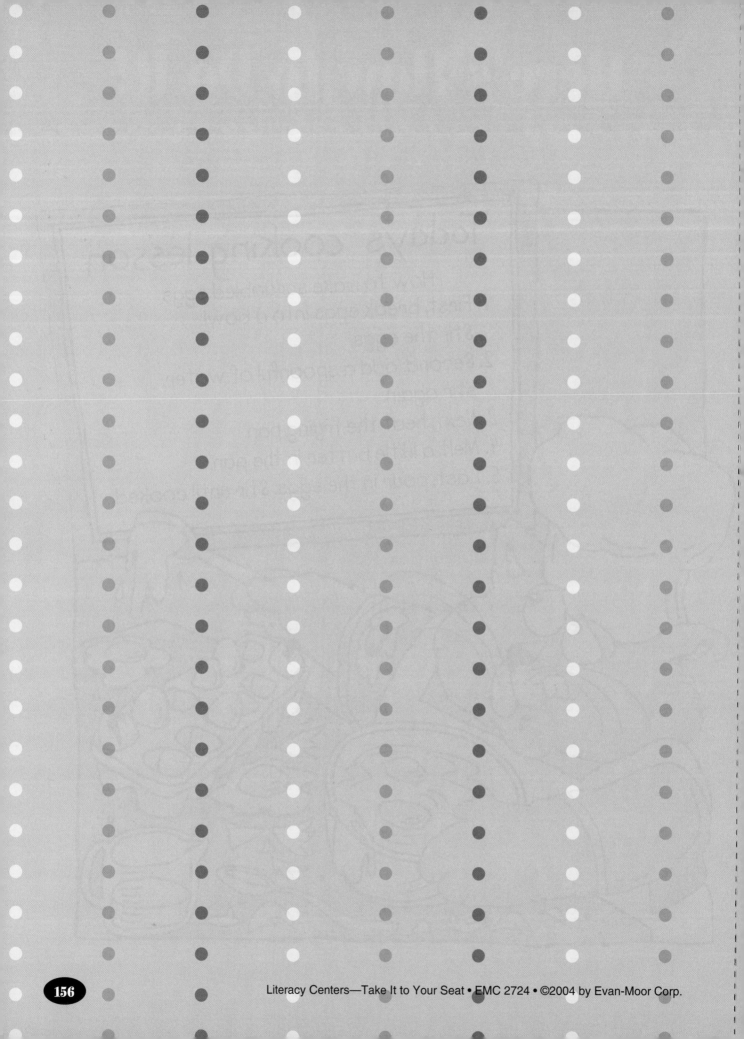

Here's How to Do It!

A **how-to paragraph** gives instructions that explain how something is done. The instructions must be in sequential, or the correct, order.

How to Make a Popsicle

First, pour juice into an ice tray. **Second**, place the ice tray into the freezer for 20 minutes. **Next**, take the tray out and stick popsicle sticks into the ice cubes. Put the tray back into the freezer until the cubes are frozen solid. **Finally**, take the tray out, turn it over, and run it under warm water. The cubes will pop out and you can enjoy your treat!

Follow these steps:

1. Choose a "how-to" task card. Write the card number on the answer form.

2. Write the steps for how to do the task on a piece of writing paper.

3. Write a paragraph that includes all the steps you've listed. Begin your paragraph by stating what it is you are explaining how to do. Then use the words *first, second, next, finally,* or *last* to introduce each step.

4. Read the paragraph. Make sure your instructions make sense. Copy the paragraph onto the answer form.

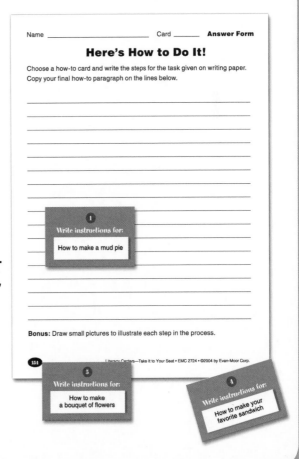

1

Write instructions for:

How to make a mud pie

2

Write instructions for:

How to make
a piece of toast

3

Write instructions for:

How to make
chocolate milk

4

Write instructions for:

How to make your
favorite sandwich

5

Write instructions for:

How to make
a bouquet of flowers

6

Write instructions for:

How to wash a dog

7

Write instructions for:

How to clean out a desk

8

Write instructions for:

How to pack for
a sleepover

Here's How to Do It!

EMC 2724
©2004 by Evan-Moor Corp.

Here's How to Do It!

EMC 2724
©2004 by Evan-Moor Corp.

Here's How to Do It!

EMC 2724
©2004 by Evan-Moor Corp.

Here's How to Do It!

EMC 2724
©2004 by Evan-Moor Corp.

Here's How to Do It!

EMC 2724
©2004 by Evan-Moor Corp.

Here's How to Do It!

EMC 2724
©2004 by Evan-Moor Corp.

Here's How to Do It!

EMC 2724
©2004 by Evan-Moor Corp.

Here's How to Do It!

EMC 2724
©2004 by Evan-Moor Corp.

9

Write instructions for:

How to paint a picture

10

Write instructions for:

How to fly a kite

11

Write instructions for:

How to ride a bike

12

Write instructions for:

How to catch a baseball

13

Write instructions for:

How to wash dirty dishes

14

Write instructions for:

How to plant a seed

15

Write instructions for:

How to take care
of a goldfish

16

Write instructions for:

How to make an
ice-cream sundae

Here's How to Do It!

EMC 2724
©2004 by Evan-Moor Corp.

Here's How to Do It!

EMC 2724
©2004 by Evan-Moor Corp.

Here's How to Do It!

EMC 2724
©2004 by Evan-Moor Corp.

Here's How to Do It!

EMC 2724
©2004 by Evan-Moor Corp.

Here's How to Do It!

EMC 2724
©2004 by Evan-Moor Corp.

Here's How to Do It!

EMC 2724
©2004 by Evan-Moor Corp.

Here's How to Do It!

EMC 2724
©2004 by Evan-Moor Corp.

Here's How to Do It!

EMC 2724
©2004 by Evan-Moor Corp.

Making Sense of Sentences

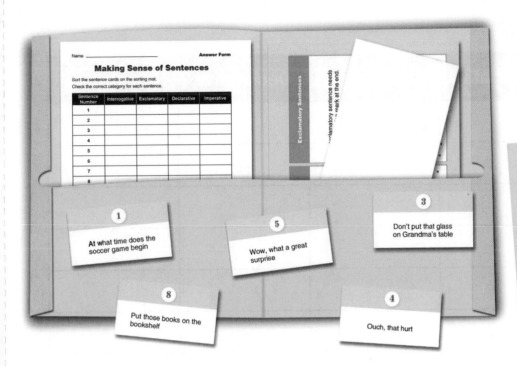

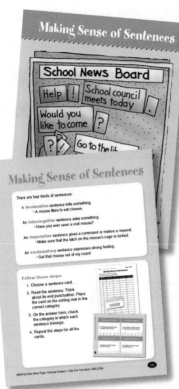

Preparing the Center

1. Prepare a folder following the directions on page 3.

   Cover—page 165
   Student Directions—page 167
   Sorting Mat—page 169
   Task Cards—pages 171 and 173

2. Reproduce a supply of the answer form on page 164. Place copies in the left-hand pocket of the folder.

Using the Center

1. The student takes an answer form and selects a sentence card.

2. The student classifies the sentence by placing it in the correct category on the sorting mat.

3. The student sorts all of the sentences.

4. For each sentence, the student checks the appropriate category on the answer form.

Name _____   **Answer Form**

Making Sense of Sentences

Sort the sentence cards on the sorting mat.

Check the correct category for each sentence.

Sentence Number	Interrogative	Exclamatory	Declarative	Imperative
1				
2				
3				
4				
5				
6				
7				
8				
9				
10				
11				
12				
13				
14				
15				
16				

Bonus: Write one more sentence in each category.

Literacy Centers—Take It to Your Seat • EMC 2724 • ©2004 by Evan-Moor Corp.

Making Sense of Sentences

There are four kinds of sentences:

A **declarative** sentence tells something.
- A mouse likes to eat cheese.

An **interrogative** sentence asks something.
- Have you ever seen a real mouse?

An **imperative** sentence gives a command or makes a request.
- Make sure that the latch on the mouse's cage is locked.

An **exclamatory** sentence expresses strong feeling.
- Get that mouse out of my room!

Follow these steps:

1. Choose a sentence card.

2. Read the sentence. Think about its end punctuation. Place the card on the sorting mat in the correct category.

3. On the answer form, check the category in which each sentence belongs.

4. Repeat the steps for all the cards.

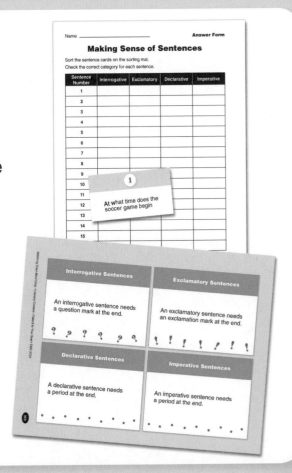

Exclamatory Sentences

An exclamatory sentence needs an exclamation mark at the end.

Imperative Sentences

An imperative sentence needs a period at the end.

Interrogative Sentences

An interrogative sentence needs a question mark at the end.

Declarative Sentences

A declarative sentence needs a period at the end.

Making Sense of Sentences
Sorting Mat

1	**2**
At what time does the soccer game begin	Let's meet at the park for practice
3	**4**
Don't put that glass on Grandma's table	Ouch, that hurt
5	**6**
Wow, what a great surprise	Carlos and Ana went to Mexico
7	**8**
Can you explain how to do this problem	Put those books on the bookshelf

Making Sense of Sentences

EMC 2724
©2004 by Evan-Moor Corp.

Making Sense of Sentences

EMC 2724
©2004 by Evan-Moor Corp.

Making Sense of Sentences

EMC 2724
©2004 by Evan-Moor Corp.

Making Sense of Sentences

EMC 2724
©2004 by Evan-Moor Corp.

Making Sense of Sentences

EMC 2724
©2004 by Evan-Moor Corp.

Making Sense of Sentences

EMC 2724
©2004 by Evan-Moor Corp.

Making Sense of Sentences

EMC 2724
©2004 by Evan-Moor Corp.

Making Sense of Sentences

EMC 2724
©2004 by Evan-Moor Corp.

9	10
At what time does the meeting begin	I can't wait for vacation

11	12
The frightened dog hid under the porch	Where is Margo's kitten

13	14
Please carry your plate to the kitchen	I was scared out of my mind

15	16
Can you come to a sleepover	My goodness, that is a huge cockroach

One Word–Two Meanings

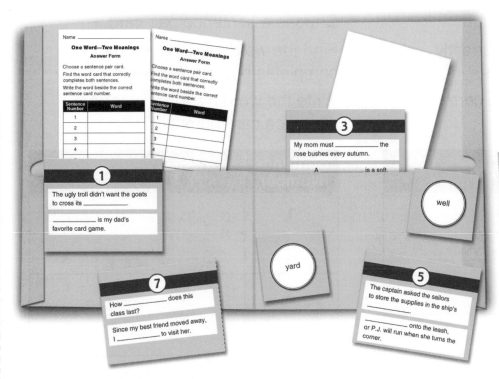

Preparing the Center

1. Prepare a folder following the directions on page 3.

   Cover—page 177
   Student Directions—page 179
   Task Cards—pages 181–187

2. Reproduce a supply of the answer form on page 176. Place copies in the left-hand pocket of the folder.

Using the Center

1. The student takes an answer form, selects a sentence pair card, and finds a word card that correctly completes both of the sentences.

2. The student writes the word on the answer form next to the correct sentence card number.

Name _____

One Word—Two Meanings
Answer Form

Choose a sentence pair card.

Find the word card that correctly completes both sentences.

Write the word beside the correct sentence card number.

Sentence Number	Word
1	
2	
3	
4	
5	
6	
7	
8	
9	
10	
11	
12	

Bonus: On the back of this form, write two sentences that use different meanings for each of these words:

bit   count   mean

Name _____

One Word—Two Meanings
Answer Form

Choose a sentence pair card.

Find the word card that correctly completes both sentences.

Write the word beside the correct sentence card number.

Sentence Number	Word
1	
2	
3	
4	
5	
6	
7	
8	
9	
10	
11	
12	

Bonus: On the back of this form, write two sentences that use different meanings for each of these words:

bit   count   mean

Literacy Centers—Take It to Your Seat • EMC 2724 • ©2004 by Evan-Moor Corp.

One Word–Two Meanings

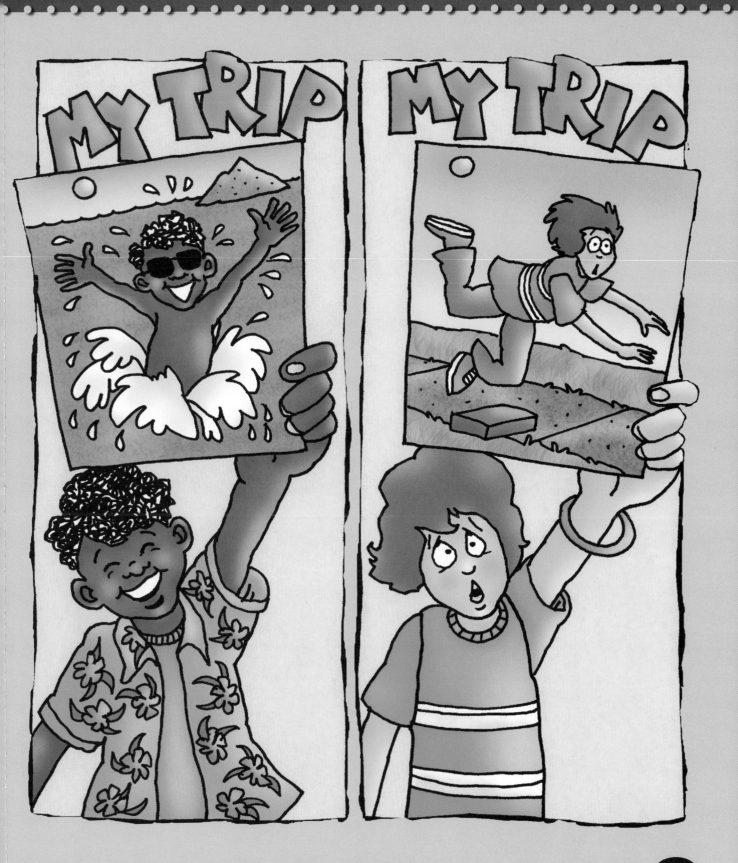

One Word–Two Meanings

Many words have more than one meaning. These words are called **multiple-meaning words**.

Follow these steps:

1. Choose a numbered sentence pair card.

2. Find the word card that correctly completes both of the sentences.

3. On the answer form, write the word next to the correct sentence card number.

4. Repeat the steps for all the cards.

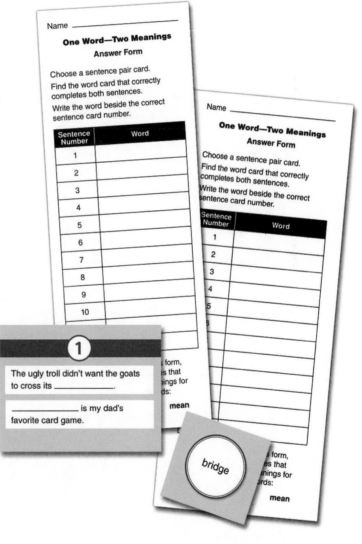

3

My mom must _____ the rose bushes every autumn.

A _____ is a soft, sweet fruit that looks like a big raisin.

4

During the fire drill, every class walks carefully in a single _____.

Mrs. Watson keeps corrected papers in the homework _____.

1

The ugly troll didn't want the goats to cross its _____.

_____ is my dad's favorite card game.

2

The bell is Mrs. Beckman's _____ to dismiss the class.

That long, thin stick with the felt tip is called a pool _____.

One Word–Two Meanings
Sentence Pair Card

One Word–Two Meanings
Sentence Pair Card

One Word–Two Meanings
Sentence Pair Card

One Word–Two Meanings
Sentence Pair Card

7

How _____ does this class last?

Since my best friend moved away, I _____ to visit her.

8

I don't like meat when it's red, so I never order my hamburger _____.

The stamp on the old envelope was very _____.

5

The captain asked the sailors to store the supplies in the ship's _____.

_____ onto the leash, or P.J. will run when she turns the corner.

6

Mark's Grandma makes a jar of strawberry _____ every year.

The school bus was stuck in a traffic _____ for over an hour.

One Word–Two Meanings
Sentence Pair Card

One Word–Two Meanings
Sentence Pair Card

One Word–Two Meanings
Sentence Pair Card

One Word–Two Meanings
Sentence Pair Card

11

I threw a penny in the wishing _____.

I hope that Mr. Evans is feeling _____ today.

12

Susan bought one _____ of cotton fabric.

My dog stays outside in the _____ while I'm at school.

9

I had a flat _____ on my bike.

I wonder if my little brother will ever _____ of playing with blocks.

10

There is a zigzag design on the _____ of his shoe.

He was the _____ survivor of the crash.

One Word–Two Meanings
Sentence Pair Card

One Word–Two Meanings
Sentence Pair Card

One Word–Two Meanings
Sentence Pair Card

One Word–Two Meanings
Sentence Pair Card

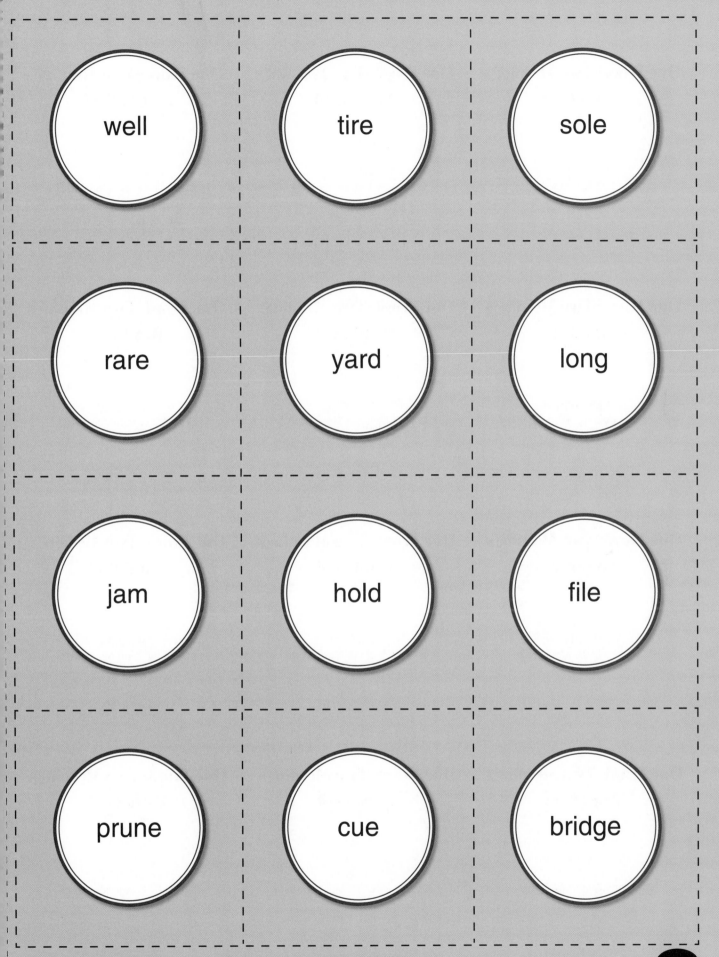

well

tire

sole

rare

yard

long

jam

hold

file

prune

cue

bridge

One Word–Two Meanings Word Card

EMC 2724
©2004 by Evan-Moor Corp.

One Word–Two Meanings Word Card

EMC 2724
©2004 by Evan-Moor Corp.

One Word–Two Meanings Word Card

EMC 2724
©2004 by Evan-Moor Corp.

One Word–Two Meanings Word Card

EMC 2724
©2004 by Evan-Moor Corp.

One Word–Two Meanings Word Card

EMC 2724
©2004 by Evan-Moor Corp.

One Word–Two Meanings Word Card

EMC 2724
©2004 by Evan-Moor Corp.

One Word–Two Meanings Word Card

EMC 2724
©2004 by Evan-Moor Corp.

One Word–Two Meanings Word Card

EMC 2724
©2004 by Evan-Moor Corp.

One Word–Two Meanings Word Card

EMC 2724
©2004 by Evan-Moor Corp.

One Word–Two Meanings Word Card

EMC 2724
©2004 by Evan-Moor Corp.

One Word–Two Meanings Word Card

EMC 2724
©2004 by Evan-Moor Corp.

One Word–Two Meanings Word Card

EMC 2724
©2004 by Evan-Moor Corp.

Answer Key

Students' answers will not necessarily be in the same order as the answer key.

Page 5 What Does It Mean?

Set 1

persevered—to keep trying and not give up, even when it's difficult

tedious—boring and repetitious

dismal—dark and gloomy

strenuous—requiring a lot of strength and energy

consequence—what happens as a result of another action

commence—to begin

convenient—useful, easy, and no trouble

thorough—careful and complete

Set 2

dilemma—difficult choice

destitute—without food, shelter, or money

stagnant—not active, changing, or developing

defiant—standing up against someone or something

ingenious—clever or skillful

renovate—to make like new

conceal—to hide, disguise, or keep secret

tolerate—to be able to put up with something

Page 17 How Many Syllables?

Set 1

1-syllable words: said, none

2-syllable words: football, about, because, practice, female, merchant

3-syllable words: excellent, terrible, already, chocolate

4-syllable words: category, testimony

5-syllable words: curiosity, university

6-syllable words: responsibility, availability

Bonus: Students should add two pairs of words. The words on the right side should total more syllables.

Set 2

1-syllable words: fold, heard

2-syllable words: forty, often, writing, surprise, address, birthday

3-syllable words: principal, tomorrow, medicine, difficult

4-syllable words: everybody, acceptable

5-syllable words: representative, sophisticated

6-syllable words: incomprehensible, underestimated

Bonus: Students should add two pairs of words. The words on the right side should total more syllables.

Set 3

1-syllable words: your, bought

2-syllable words: balloon, people, answered, sometime

3-syllable words: favorite, traveling, computer, handkerchief

4-syllable words: capitalize, certificate, explanation, calamity

5-syllable words: cafeteria, pronunciation

6-syllable words: experimentation, inferiority

Bonus: Students should add two pairs of words. The words on the right side should total more syllables.

Page 29 Draw...Then Write a Story

Students' writing will vary.

Page 41 Name the Relationship

Set 1

antonym:
amuse : bore :: attack : defend
awake : asleep :: after : before

cause & effect:
misbehavior : punishment ::
   oversleeping : tardy
heat : sweating :: cold : shivering

part-whole:
lens : camera :: wing : plane
nail : finger :: eyelash : eye
mouse : computer ::
   remote control : television

synonym:
plot : scheme :: pleasure : enjoyment
vacant : empty :: thief : robber
gift : present :: active : lively

Set 2

antonym:
answer : question :: alone : together
fiction : fact :: long : short

cause & effect:
push : fall :: practice : improve
earthquake : damage ::
   infection : illness
hot : boiling :: cold: freezing
run : tired :: sleep : rested

part-whole:
index : book :: eraser : pencil
lens : camera :: reel : fishing pole

synonym:
part : portion :: weak : feeble
blend : mix :: right : correct

Page 51 Where Can I Find It?

Card 1

1. Who the chapter is about, an occupation, years the person lived, and page the chapter starts on

2. She was an architect who lived from 1872 until 1957.

3. The chapter on May Arkwright Hutton begins on page 38.

4. Students should reference the common theme of women in the book. Possible answer: Women Who Helped Build America

Card 1–backside

1. There are 7 pages that contain information about the Cherokee Nation.

2. The definition of the American West is on pages 12 and 13.

3. A photograph of Evelyn Cameron is on page 129.

4. Answers will vary.

Card 2

1. The book is divided into two parts. Each part has five chapters.

2. Begin reading on page 24 to find out about descriptive details.

3. I will learn about how to choose a narrator when writing a story.

4. Chapter 6. A better place to start for specific information is the index.

Card 2–backside

1. Each of the words represents a specific topic having to do with character(s).

2. Read pages 90–96 to learn to describe the setting of a story.

3. Pages 9 and 10 are about alliteration.

4. Topics are arranged alphabetically; subtopics are alphabetical under the main topic.

Card 3

1. The subject of this book is Native American games.

2. Page 133 has Skill games.

3. There are 20 pages about Racing and Kicking games.

4. The Table of Contents references the introduction, list of illustrations, and index.

Card 3–backside

1. Pinecone Hoop Toss is a Tossing and Catching game.

2. The effects of dreams on games is on page 17.

3. Star Groups is the name of a specific game because it is capitalized.

4. The game Rebound would be added between Rattler! and Ring in a Ring.

Card 4

1. Chapter titles are all capital letters.

2. On page 26 I would read about the Indian Wars and the French and Indian rivalry.

3. I would read the geography chapter to find out about the different climatic regions in Canada.

4. Windsurfing in Canada would be in the Water Sports section, which starts on page 51.

Card 4–backside

1. The abbreviation for the Federation du Frog Lovers is FFL.

2. The names of specific people, places, and organizations (proper nouns) are capitalized.

3. The Fairview Cemetery is located in Halifax, N.S. You can read about it on page 245.

4. Pages 129–130, 267, and 269 have information on festivals in Manitoba.

Page 65 Word Pictures

Students' writing will vary.

Page 75 Groups of Three

Set 1

show / display / exhibit

habit / routine / practice

imagine / invent / create

fair / just / impartial

last / end / final

ruin / spoil / destroy

Set 2

manage / direct / supervise

necessary / needed / required

keep / own / retain

tour / trip / excursion

quick / swift / fleet

rebel / defy / resist

Page 85 Just the Opposite

Set 1

captivity / freedom

careful / haphazard

spotless / stained

rapid / slow

employed / jobless

cautious / daring

rigid / flexible

saturated / dry

restrain / release

humble / conceited

doubtful / confident

serious / comical

Set 2

fail / triumph

match / differ

stout / slender

ordinary / uncommon

preserve / waste

encourage / deter

retrieve / lose

bellow / whisper

capture / release

friendly / grouchy

tangle / unravel

durable / fragile

Page 95 What's an Idiom?

Set 1

Idiom: by the skin of your teeth
Meaning: just barely

Idiom: butterflies in the stomach
Meaning: a fluttering feeling in the stomach usually caused by nervousness

Idiom: button your lip
Meaning: be quiet

Idiom: call it a day
Meaning: stop work

Idiom: calm before the storm
Meaning: a period of peace before a disturbance

Idiom: can't see the forest for the trees
Meaning: to be so involved in details that you miss the whole picture

Set 2

Idiom: make ends meet
Meaning: earn just enough to live

Idiom: miss the boat
Meaning: lose an opportunity

Idiom: carry the ball
Meaning: make sure the job gets done right

Idiom: down the drain
Meaning: lost forever

Idiom: elbow grease
Meaning: hard, energetic effort

Idiom: scratch the surface
Meaning: to deal with only a very small part of a subject

Page 107 Two into One

Students' answers will vary. Sentences may be combined correctly in various ways.

Page 117 Fix It Up!

Letter 1

Dear Miss Muffet,

I'm writing to you from the Marvelous Tuffet Mart. We want to announce our yearly sale. Do you need a new tuffet? We have great values on both velvet and leather tuffets.

Please stop by our showroom to see our outstanding selection.

Sincerely,

The Sales Staff at Tuffet Mart

P.S. Bring this letter with you to receive a 25% discount on the tuffet of your choice.

Letter 2

Dear Jack,

The Sprout Seed Company is proud to send you a sample of our new giant bean seeds. The plant that grows from these seeds will be over 500 feet tall! The stem is sturdy for easy climbing. Please try the five seeds we have enclosed and let us know what you think.

Sincerely,

Sam at Sprout Seed Company

P.S. This new bean plant can be easily chopped down with a sharp ax!

Letter 3

Dear John,

Enclosed you will find a pair of our cozy sleep socks. Please try them and let us know whether you find them helpful. With or without shoes, they will keep your feet cozy and warm. You may purchase additional pairs at your local department store.

Yours truly,

The Sleep Staff at cozysocks.com

P.S. Additional socks are available online at **www.cozysocks.com**.

Letter 4

Dear Mary-Mary,

I understand that you are quite contrary. You may want to consider enrolling in one of our friendship classes. Even the most grumpy characters have made lasting friendships after attending our classes. I have enclosed the July schedule for your information.

Sincerely,

Professor Get-a-long Great

P.S. Enroll today and receive $200 off the cost of your class!/.

Letter 5

Dear Little Boy Blue,

Congratulations! You have won a set of horn lessons. Soon you will be blowing your favorite tunes! Call today to set up your first lesson.

Yours truly,

Mr. Music

P.S. We have a great selection of music books, too.

Letter 6

Dear Little Pigs,

We're sending you a free sample of our house plans. Next time you build a new home, follow the easy steps. Your house will be strong, and you will be safe.

Sincerely,

Master Builders

P.S. Buy your building supplies at our warehouse. We have bricks, sticks, and straw.

Page 129 Pattern a Poem

This center is an opportunity for students to be creative while following a specific poetic form.

Page 141 Get to the Root of It

ann—annual, anniversary, annuity

ast—astronaut, disaster, astronomy, asterisk

doc—doctor, doctrine, document

duc—duct, conduct, educate, aqueduct

form—uniform, transform, reform, formal

jud, jur, jus—judge, jury, justice

lab—labor, laboratory, elaborate

miss, mit—submit, remit, missile, dismiss

vac—vacant, vacation, evacuate, vacuum

Page 153 Here's How to Do It!

Students' answers will vary.

Page 163 Making Sense of Sentences

1. interrogative
2. imperative
3. imperative or exclamatory
4. exclamatory
5. exclamatory
6. declarative
7. interrogative
8. imperative
9. interrogative
10. exclamatory
11. declarative
12. interrogative
13. imperative
14. exclamatory
15. interrogative
16. exclamatory

Page 175 One Word–Two Meanings

1. bridge
2. cue
3. prune
4. file
5. hold
6. jam
7. long
8. rare
9. tire
10. sole
11. well
12. yard